PRAISE FOR *VILLAIN*

Villain's Vernacular is a tapestry of poetry and short stories that explore the struggles and hardships of the human experience, ranging from love to poverty and the daily struggles that come with it. Fueled by a central focus on the theme of villains, Ornelas' work is a thought provoking journey that is dark and insightful as it invites readers to consider the complexities of the antagonist and to look deeper into the human soul. Rich in the literary devices and forms of the poetic tradition, this collection makes for not just a read, but an experience to learn from, for both literary enthusiasts and students alike. This second poetry collection irrefutably establishes Carlos Ornelas among the most masterful poets of our time.

— Antonia 'Vela' Villegas PhD, Author/Educator

Carlos Ornelas is, quite simply, one of the greatest rhythmic poets Los Angeles has ever seen. His comprehension and execution of lyric poetry is unmatched by any poet I have ever heard. His subject matter is homegrown in LA, echoing profound verses from the other side of the tracks. Every time I get to hear or read an Ornelas poem, I sit on the edge of my seat waiting for the greatness to come, and it arrives every time, in every stanza, on every page.

— Hiram Sims, Community Literature Initiative Executive Director
& Los Angeles Library Commissioner

In this collection of poetry, Ornelas turns America's villain into the hero who fights for the poor, the immigrant, the incarcerated. The villain's vernacular is truth — his weapon of choice — which he uses to tear down the lies and institutions that keep people oppressed and subjugated. To read *Villain's Vernacular* is to resist, to free oneself from the bondage of American colonialism.

— Obed Silva, English Professor at East Los Angeles College
& author of *The Death of My Father The Pope*

VILLAIN'S VERNACULAR

VILLAIN'S VERNACULAR

POEMS & STORIES

CARLOS ORNELAS

RIOT OF ROSES
PUBLISHING HOUSE

SEJATNGA
UNCEDED TONGVA TERRITORY
SOUTH WHITTIER, CALIFORNIA

Published by Riot of Roses Publishing House

Villain's Vernacular
Copyright © 2024, Carlos Ornelas
ISBN (paperback): 978-1-961717-11-4
ISBN (hardcover): 978-1-961717-18-3
ISBN (ebook): 978-1-961717-14-5
ISBN (audio): 978-1-961717-19-0
LCCN: 2024943094

Cover Art
© 2024, Gabrijela Levakovic

First Edition, 2024

To request permissions, you may contact the Publisher at riotofrosesllc@gmail.com

Printed in the United States of America.

www.riotofrosespublishinghouse.com

Cover design by Carlos Ornelas & Emily Anne Evans
Layout design by Emily Anne Evans
Editor-in-Chief: Brenda Vaca

To the world of Literature, Poetry, and Words.

To the world of Music and Art.

For the preservation and advancement of thought, artistry, creativity, and the collective Human experience.

For all who can relate.

CONTENTS

CHAPTER 3: UNSCRUPULOUS MOTIVES

CHAPTER 4: ANTIHERO

CHAPTER 5: HARDHEARTED

CHAPTER 6: VILLAIN

*Short Story

PREFACE

Before you begin your journey into this book, you should know that these pages that you hold before you have saved my life. How did this book save my life? By means of keeping me occupied on something positive: the writing courses and workshops and the open mics I participated in and the features and readings I've done and conventions I've attended while making this book kept me focused on something positive while dealing with a negative subject. Writing the material for this book caused me to better understand living and its countless complexities. I produced this book in efforts to combine my empathy and my creativity. I crafted this book as an opportunity to challenge the Western literary canon and establish an outlook on life that is less ethnocentric and less patriarchal and more universal and accessible and relatable to all. I made this book to be read, to be studied, or to be ignored like so many other books we humans construct for the wrong reasons. I've rid myself of that bothersome guilt by making a book that is not meant for anyone but to save myself because our survival instinct is selfish by nature, but in doing so, I've created an object that can also be utilized by those who are looking to find a sense of belonging to this world as I have. I've rid myself of the burden of making a best seller or a book worthy of an award, or an honorable mention. This is simply a book of poems and stories, that may or may not help you, as they have helped me.

Why write this book and who is it written for? Though this book was not written for any audience in particular, I inadvertently composed this book for the children who were never granted a fair opportunity at success. For the people who get treated as less by the general public. For the people who are not considered a priority in our human society. For all of us who someone deems as less important than the vast majority. This is for the underdog who is portrayed as the anti-hero by the actual villain. For the kids who were always told that they would amount to nothing, or who were constantly told were "Bad Kids." For the children who have never experienced someone say to them that they are exceptional and that it's going to be alright. Just because they exhibit bad behavior does not make them bad. For everyone discriminated against, or treated unjustly, at school, at a job interview, or at church. Because of the way you look or the way you think, the words you speak or the ideology you believe in. For all of those people and for anyone who finds some sustenance in my work. I wrote this book to all those who find comfort in my words or for those who are just interested in the stories from the other side of the tracks.

Putting this book together was a learning experience that taught me lots about the world of publishing books, the world of poetry and the world of writing stories. It has been a journey that has allowed me to meet so many wonderful poets, activists, writers and artists, and some of them have become family to me.

I wrote this book because life has made me an expert on the subject of mishap. I wrote this book because I needed to tell these stories and no one else will tell them like I can.

Carlos Ornelas
Long Beach, California
Saturday, November 4, 2023
2:22 am

.

INTRODUCTION

Welcome to a poetic tapestry woven with shades of darkness. Where the wicked and misunderstood take center stage. Enter a world where villains become the heroes of their own stories. Delve into a realm where the lines blur between good and evil. Step into the shadows where darkness dances with poetry. Take a tour of the underworld that lies beneath the streetlights beyond those freeway offramps you've never dared to exit after midnight. Travel deep within the parameters, lairs, hideouts, headquarters and hangouts, and visualize existence through the eyes of the underprivileged. These pages will challenge how you look at villains by presenting a glance inside the mind of a villain through the most intimate form of expression of said villain: his words. What is *Villain's Vernacular*? It is that which encompasses the world of a villain and ultimately identifies him or her as one. It is the language used by people to communicate with one another within their own communities. It is the music they identify with, the culture they grew up embracing. Vernacular is the language and/ or culture that identifies a specific group of people. Therefore, villain's vernacular is the language, culture and characteristics that identifies and classifies a group of people as villains. Unlike conventional tales, this story begins with its most important character: the villain.

VILLAIN'S VERNACULAR

CHAPTER 1

ANTAGONIST

The Opposite of Positive

*. . . Then, from out of the bluest left field,
came some malicious villain.*

Man 1: *Oh yea? And what did the people do?*

Man 2: *They ran like a bat out of hell!*

Man 1: *And what did you do?*

Man 2: *Nothing, I was the Malicious Villain.*

A Villain's Introduction

Hello, I am me.
You will meet me and perhaps you will not dislike me more.
I am he who transforms venom into medicine.
Cat into elephant
Anunnaki at the Compton swap meet.
Aren't we all shooting stars or falling stars?...
I don't know who you came with homie,
But these words are mine.
Feel free to take as many of them as you'd like,
I'm turning songs into bullets now.
My poems have been poisoned.
Devenomized and milked.
When victims also carry guilt,
man-made guilt,
custom quilt.
As soon as we took the chains off we wanna put them back on.
Who taught me this cruel and weak mentality of the meek?
I am only villain to those who wish me so;
to others: brothers
my enemies don't dress like me.
Light up spliffs instead of incense,
for the king of all the insects,
go ahead and point your index,
you tell me what you see
when they distort your reality.

Renaissance

Rhyme concocting
Poem constructing
Story telling me.

Cigarette smoking, Child raising, improper English speaking,
deep thinking me.
Tax paying, non-vaccinated, Joint in the ear,
homemade studio sound engineer.
Hip-hop critic, fake repellent, faith heal medic, selfless me.

Men's central jail no bail, 7th man in a 6 man cell,
femme fatale male, Narcan man at a fentanyl festival,
somewhat dependable, Despicable me.
Higher caliber character, my pen is Excalibur,
my speech and my stride is iambic pentameter, this is me.

English Major failure, graffiti curator, beats and rhymes,
beans and rice, Jesus Christ tomb raider, Mexican American me.

Indigenous first generation integration of immigrants,
lyrical official non artificial intelligent me.

Descendent of Olmecs, Toltecs, Nahuatl and European invaders,
lost tribe of Israel, Issachar, Isabel.

Suicide lives in me, inside this misshaped temple that really isn't me.
Temporary as a Christmas tree, poetry visits me, sits with me,
kisses me, christened me. This is me.

Baptized in fire water, holy water, PCP.
I be a spick Malcolm X and a Paisa Easy E.

Like my homey D'Lo he the black Chalino Sanchez,
He got black thoughts and a brown subconscious.

What if the pharaohs were braceros,
drive-by's were horse carriage ride-by's with obsidian arrows.

I am the advancement of *huevos rancheros*
and the result of *hueros rateros.*
Moctezuma's revenge in the form of *chiles habaneros.*
The rebirth of Aztec, refuse the casket, the new school pachuco,
the emperor's new clothes are zoot suits. This is me.

Gangbanging on the G.O.V. I'm a mean O.G.
but they try to play me like a D.O.G.,
they ask me where I'm from, I'm from G.O.D.
with a G.T.A. and a D.U.I. by age 23.
Fuck the I.N.S. and the I.C.E., tell them I got a tech like I.T.T.
Who was the first wetback to cross the ocean blue,
Christopher Columbus in 1492.
Legal aliens invading L.O.S., Angeles, send out an S.O.S.
and an A.P.B., this is me, The Renaissance of Chicano Poetry.

Waiting

...

Impatience becomes the norm.
Unread messages and missed calls
from potential clientele begin to pile up.
Creating a virtual traffic jam
of radio frequent road-rage
on misinformation highway...
Monetary fragments are accompanied by
paranoia and uncertainty.
Everyone is suspect.
Even the dirty children playing in sunshine'd alleys.
We wait...
for the plastic wrapped,
small package to arrive.
Which contains the diamond crumbs
and pebbles of temporary joy.
We wait... unsettled and reclined
on Pontiac seats.
Examining fractions of the world around us
through rear and side view mirrors...
We wait.
But it is worth the wait
when we finally acquire it.
Two and a half cigarettes later
a rough face with squinting eyes
and cicatrized smile, appears from
the rear gate of the hospital scrub baby blue project building.
He enters the vehicle through the shotgun door.
Score. Twelve point four
is the tale from a digital scale...

Benjamin Franklin times two
in exchange for the crystal blue persuasion.
A sandwich bag of glaziers,
and icicles, and spears.
Give my best to the misses
and treasure the kisses.
For they are the loyal
who visit the prisons.
Nice doing business.
Door panel removed briefly
to stash this completely,
Put it back neatly.
For poverty destined,
a peasant's investment.
For everyone loves and pays to employ
the services rendered and meant to enjoy.
Twenty-dollar bags of 'getaway' and
temporary joy.
Ethics issues not worth debating,
when the customers are waiting.
What ever happened to our dreams?
No one ever says, 'I want to sell drugs when I grow up.'
It is imposed and forced to do,
waiting...
We wait...
For dreams to come true.

PBJ

how to fill the void of the unemployed, uneducated, financially insecure
how does one fight holiday materialism
and schemes of marketing commercialism,
when every kid in school has an iPhone except yours.
how does a parent with integrity deal with the disability of poverty
during these industrialized, economized holiday seasons.
what are the reasons—why they are pimping baby Jesus,
and Santa Claus prostitutes himself at shopping malls.

why o why is the apple of my eye
a pod, a pad, a phone, a crime?
the number one reported stolen item in America is the iPhone.
not because it is a small and amazing listening device,
not because it's helping kids become better people,
not because it's nice;
it's the price. the price, the worth, the retail value is around $1000,
which in street value is anywhere from $100 to $500 cash
Apple corporation makes the best innovations of time,
or are their billion-dollar creations factors of crime.
burglary and theft are highest at Christmas time.
'tis the season of giving and taking. because the iPhone 12
is the greatest innovation of the year
until the iPhones 13 appear.
if the iPhone is such a marvelous and intelligent device,
why does it only last one year.
and then you gotta buy a new version of it?
did we miss a meeting? did we not receive the memo?
are we headed for the era of i? the iTimes?
where iCops are needed for iCrimes?
for iTheft and iFrauds? Pray to the iGods.

we are letting them get away with too much.
we've conformed and uniformed and cooperated with iCrimes
and committed secondhand iSins
and left our children bobbing for rotten apples in the dark
in a swimming pool of mercury
while we stand in line outside Best Buys and Walmart and Target.
when we are the target, for black Friday's, black market
and Christmas became a pimpstress
in a world where a parent with no job
must rob an iPhone for their child to smile and feel loved.
what happened to the holiday seasons?
they are pimping baby Jesus.

Radio, Radio

You wanna talk about democracy?
Check this out.
L.A. County holding tanks are beds
and toilet paper rolls are pillows.
And chow time, count time, and downtime,
is how time Is divided. Within these walls,
slavery has never been abolished.
In fact, it only has been polished.
Racism is promised and accomplished.
And segregation is the common knowledge.
It is the purgatory of humanity.
Where abnormality becomes reality.
An abstraction to Picasso's satisfaction.
Every action has reaction.
And the laws of Newton, definitely fashioned,
and practiced, on a daily basis.
In these mazes. And every race is racist.
While every single face in this place,
faces cases. Even those outside the cages.
Uniformed and paid in wages.
L.A. County, baptized in numerology.
So, your name is now spelled in digits.
And those who lacked the faith, have suddenly become religious.
And plagiarism of prayer, is a process,
for the criminals on crosses.
Who wonder why the misses never visits?
And the verdict doesn't end behind these bars.
Out there, they give you time.
In here, they give you scars. And jackets
that you cannot remove.

I Woke Up as a Lyricist

Composed prose,
Poems ooze out my fingertips
A tongue that is Xmas for clitoris'
Syllabus of syllabi
Substance in my stanzas,
Soliloquies, sonnets, sentences
Haikus for breakfast
Battle raps for brunch
I put a chapbook together by the time it's lunch
I called it rise and shine poetry
I spit licks for practice to give my tactics advantage
With language to vanquish the average catfish
Linguistic, my tongue is twisted, misfit—
Artistic prolific
Horrific Hieroglyphic
Script Scripted encrypted
Encoded, my codex decoded
My rap flows are fractals
The methods to madness
Weapons of language
Woke up as a lyricist
My words became images
And everything rhymes if I wish it so...
I got this vicious flow and let them bitches know
Somebody dragged cat shit up in the kitchen floor
And I'm out of *Fabuloso*, so
And when I say bitches, I'm referring to my dogs.
My dogs Candice and Sarah, that's my bitches though,
My lingo is hard to Kinko,
It's sort of like a mixture

Of Spanglish, the tongue-slang, motherland's most distinguished
Broken and refurbished English
My Spanish is famished
Of language, slang though is savage
Woke up as a lyricist
Like spirits from pyramids
Like 'Lord is you hearing this?'
Of course, you are hearing this
Holy Ghost writer of lyricists
Master puppeteer and ventriloquist
Silhouettes requesting cigarettes.
Once in a while I welcome ignorance
I woke up as a lyricist.

A Pocho With a Social

I'm not from Mexico nor from the United States.
Though I was born in L.A. I've never been treated like an American.
Only when I'm in Mexico. My *Madre patria* doesn't want me and
my mother country treats me like an adopted child.
Pocho. I laugh at the notion.
I creep in between the shadows of borders,
with pesos and quarters in my pocket.
I am the hated beaner up in White Ville USA
and the despised pocho down in Jalisco.
Paisas say I can't work for shit.
And Whites say I'm taking their jobs.
They both call me criminal and thief.
They hate my gang slang and my rap music.
But none of them take me under their wing
and show me the way of their culture.
Instead, I follow the culture of the street.
All streets and hoods and ghettos welcome me.
My culture is that of gangs, graffiti, crime and poverty.
My heroes are Tupac, Chalino Sanchez, and Tony Montana.
They say I'm uncultured. But my culture is that of Speedy Gonzales,
Danny Trejo and the clown from Fools Gone Wild,
and maybe Wilmer Valderrama,
or Mario Lopez. Whittier Blvd and Norwalk Square.
Plazita Olvera, Plaza Mexico and Nike Cortez,
the Raiders, and Homies action figures,
Victory Outreach Cholos
and the bad use of the English and Spanish languages.
A Pocho with a social, I watch Don Francisco and the Price is Right
Walter Mercado and Diane Warwick.
I am Joaquin and Sandra Cisneros.

I am huevos rancheros and twisted *dedos*,
throwing up hoods like elbows.
I am gang related *abuelos* sipping Modelos.
I am Delahoya's, Chavez, Canelo's,
I am tagging crews; Ben Davis, never could afford tattoos by cartoon.
Cheech was my substitute teacher. And Chaka was my inspiration.
My heroes disowned me and never wanted to know me.
The Mecha club and brown berets never cared to look my way.
A Pocho with a social. My big sisters were Jenni Rivera and Selena
and Snow Tha Product, Jessie Reyez,
all these chicks I'm really proud of.
I am the new Pablo Neruda running from the *jura*.
my mom smells of ruda and my bro smells of Buddha
and my sis smells of *pintura de uña*. My pop smells like *cruda*
my *padrino* sells *pura*. Pocho with a social,
Sunday night oldies Art Laboe show.
Mexican Guatemalan Salvadorian Cuban Boricua
Honduran Dominican Colombian
Argentinian Peruvian Nicaraguan Panamanian Chileno.
I'm in the corner like Tito Carlos Santana in the ghetto,
Vicente Eddie Guerrero.
Rey Mysterio of the barrio, Rosario Dawson. I'm a virgin in the closet.
Dora the Explorer's gang related cousin.
I'm a cockfighter for cockblockers
and cocker spaniel colonizers.
I am a lost cause, culture loss, Tekashi 69 nailed on a cross.
Rainbow haired, thorn crowned, Gees up, hoes down,
penitentiary bound by honor: blood in blood out,
vato loco local with the focal vocal. Little puppet, little Moco.
you can call me on my cell phone, you can call me collect,
you can call me whatever the fuck, just don't call me Pocho.

Name Brand

The worst thing and best thing about fame
is the fact that everybody knows your name.
Many times, in my life where I never been exceptional
or special or worthy of remembrance
I was in fact nameless.
A phantasm of haunted pavements
where walls scream my name in black paint
to be famous.

In the land of monthly payments and lovely pagans,
aerosol paint's bitter fragrance,
Jehovah witnesses and plaintiffs
all must know what my name is.
My peers' magnetically contagious avid admiration for Daytons,
I was immune to it.
My temporary addiction was permanent ink.
While other teens had a passion for chain-snatchin',
I was name-slashin'.
Those who crossed out my name, in the same fashion,
on dark autumn nights I'd visit their hood
like the joker up in Bruce Wayne's mansion.

Now my enemies' uncharted terrain has been desecrated
and tattooed with my name,
my alias, my AKA, my street name.
Striving for a spot in the halls of street fame.
It is quite strange to remain a nameless entity
while having a famous secret identity.
And when my enemies finally came around
searching for my name, it was me that they found.
The best thing and worst thing about fame
is the fact that everybody knows your name brand.

The Thanksgiving Dinner Guest

Small talk at the dinner table on Thanksgiving.
One of the guests says he is a software developer for Microsoft;
the other is a contractor in the union.
And the other owns a subway restaurant.
The other drives a tow truck.
And you? What do you do?
Well damn, I command words for a living.
I conduct words, and syllables.
I build stanzas, to make couplets, with ballpoint pens.
I architect quatrains with black ink and number two pencils.
I ghostwrite for R&B female singers,
and Latin jazz groups. I'm a script engineer.
I convert beats into songs,
I'm an audio architect.
I build foundations and bridges,
out of forty-eight bars and three hooks.
I'm a poetry scientist, a theatrical technician.
A Designer of diction. Archbishop of this lyrical religion.
Dictionary physician, encyclopedia-trition.
I'm a verse Villain. Me, versus, the universes.
I got words, like foreign films with subtitles.
What do you do?
I'm an attorney for Larry H. Parker and you?
I'm a truck driver for Albertsons, and you?
I'm a registered nurse for Kaiser Permanente,
and you, I'm a regional manager for Wells Fargo,
and you, what do you do?
Me? I write dope shit.
I fill up composition book pages, front and back.

I write constitutions for Community College
associated student body organizations.
I write real, real shit.
I write prayers for angels.
I write operas for tenors.
I write plays about Shakespeare.
I write radio commercials for DOS EQUIS.
I write jokes for politicians.
I write policies and odysseys,
and I'm working on my third epic.
I write haikus and battle raps.
I got notebooks, the size of phonebooks.
I write success stories of homies from the hood that made it.
I write draft Scriptures, and words that paint pictures.
Just in case Jesus comes back next year
and starts to hire people to write for the new, New Testament.
I'm rewriting my resume, to apply for Judgment Day,
As a writer, for the new Bible's Revival.
And turn in my application for apostle, disciple.
What do you do?
I'm a LAPD police officer, and you?
I'm a dental assistant.
I am a social worker for the county of Los Angeles, and you?
Pass the mashed potatoes and gravy, please. Thank you.
Who me?
I write.
My name is Carlos. Nice to meet you.
And I am the one who wrote this poem.

Where Do I Stand

why am I afraid
of becoming a slave
in the land of the free
and the home of the brave
brave, brave, like the children who remain caged
till this day because they're undocumented parents were deported
brave, brave, brave,
like single parents who raise children to be great
despite gangster role models
whose throat takes swallows from patron bottles
brave like my mother with a basket
picking peaches in a field full of sexist men
brave, brave,
like Emmett Till's mother before the grave
brave like MLK on his death day walking up to podiums
brave, brave,
like Shirley Chisholm in '68
first Black congresswoman in the United States
brave
like Tommy Smith and John Carlos
taking first and third place in the 200-meter race
with power fist raised during the Olympic Games
brave
like Mexican ladies who push grocery carts
with corn on sticks and a bra full of 20s
in a poor, poor neighborhood
brave, brave,
like immigrants crossing borders
in the back of 18 Wheelers
not knowing if they will ever again

see the light of day
brave
like runaway slaves running across plantations and graves
and rather get caught and killed than to remain enslaved
brave
like Cesar Chavez doing speeches and leading hunger strikes
that boycotted grapes in support of migrant workers who are grossly
underpaid
brave
like young brown women who were raped
and must face the same rapist on a court date
land of the free, free, like Mumia ain't
free like public defenders who pretend to represent me
free like restitution fees
free like bald Eagles in Yosemite
free like our ancestors could never be
free like my speech and water are supposed to be
free like you and I pretend to be
free
this land of the free
home of the brave
but why am I afraid
of becoming a slave
when I'm supposed to be free, free, free,
in this land, one ordinary man
in this land, where my sister got blisters in her hand
and they paid my people pennies since the 1920s
in this land, where you think you're American
till you can't attend the same schools that Harry and Kelly can
in this land

where it's harder for a kid to join a band
and easier to join a gang.
in this land,
land of the free
home of the brave
where I am afraid
of becoming a slave
land of the free
home of the brave,
of the brave,
the brave,
brave, brave,
in this land,
where do I stand?

Worth

What's the price of art
What's the price of fame
What's it worth having
the world knowing your name?

How much for your art
How much does it cost
Do you own the rights
Or should I talk to your boss?

Is it really yours?
Maybe it never was
Maybe you made it
but now it belongs to us.

Do you love your craft
enough to keep it hid
so no one ever knows
all the beauty that you did?

Remember as a kid
Never was the smartest
Only most honest
Enough to be an artist.

But tell me what's the purpose?
To do the world a service?
Ungrateful motherfuckers
They got you feeling worthless.

But you know what your worth is
even at those events
Where nobody shows up
No clients or no friends

And it don't even matter
You're still going through it
Clients or your friends
ain't the reason why you do it.

I do it cause I'm human
And cause I'm going through it
But all these mutherfuckers
think I do it just to do it

And many of them ruined
the beauty you compose
the pictures that you paint
the truth that you expose

Maybe you were chosen
to show and lead the way
And one day we'll appreciate
everything you say

And what's the price to pay
Will you play the part
What's the part you play
to get paid for the art?

Do it with your heart
With a heart of gold
is worth much more
than everything you sold

But never sold your soul
you sold a couple pieces
and still stole the show
with all your new releases

I'm sitting in the bleachers
admiring the teachers
imagining one day
I'll be one of your features

What's the price of art
Tell me what is worth
How much does it cost
Or should I talk to your boss?

What's the price of art?

Our Heroes Have Failed Us

If our Gods worked for the government
Instead of prayers we would submit petitions
For Heaven to help us

God would have created the world
In seven business days
Every four millennia humanity would elect its new lord and savior

People would hold signs that say
"Catholics for Christ"
"Mohammed for Vice"
"Choose hey Zeus"

"Allah can't lose"
We are the welfare children of Captain America
Adopted by Dr. Doom.

Our heroes have failed us
They've taken the credit
For crosses that nailed us
They act as if patriots just to befriend us

Then they enslave us, sell us, or shelve us,
If our Gods worked for the government
Heaven would allow only National Citizens
All others considered illegal spirits

Guardian Angels: National guards
Label our world as a Paradise Lost
Instead of Gods, in guns we would trust
And wear an M-16 Instead of a cross

If our Gods worked for the government
Every tax season would be an apocalypse
Instead of Saint Peter: George Stephanopoulos
Monica Lewinsky: The new Mary Magdalene

Abortions instead of conceptions immaculate
If our Gods worked for the government
Committing sins would lead to fines
And up to two years in purgatory

And if you wanted to repent
You would need to hire a patron Saint
To plead in your defense
If our Gods worked for the government

But in reality, our governments don't work
Because God does not work for the Government
May heaven help us
Our heroes have failed us

THE BIPOLAR EXPRESS: ACT 1

Some things are meant to be forgotten but I will always keep alive the very moment, of the first time I killed a living thing. I must have been 5 years old. I was playing near a big pine tree outside of my mother's house in Mexico, and I happened to find a fallen nest. I looked inside the nest, and I found a circled white rock with little brown spots on it. I picked up the small rock and held it in between the index and thumb fingers on my right hand. I brought it closer to my eyes to examine the smooth shape of this rock, as I held it tightly and squinted my right eye and closed my left one, crack! Gooey yellowish slimy liquid mixed with blood and clear mucus-like fluid squirts on my nose, eyebrows and the inside of my lip. It was an egg. And it held a baby embryo inside, who now lies dormant in between my two fingers. It moves slightly its little unformed pink wing. Then it stops. It dies. From that day forward I knew an irrefutable exceptional truth: I can kill.

I am a one-way passenger on the ever-fluctuating train of life. En route to who knows where. I am on this carcinogenic train in which I first boarded in the Los Angeles Winter of 1978. December first in fact, a Friday. Currently, I am 8 years old, but time works differently aboard this train. Sometimes, the days seem like minutes and what you thought was an hour or two is actually a year or two.

I look out the window but all I see is my reflection. It is night. We will arrive to my first destination, childhood, in the morning hours. This is the place where I will drop off the innocence I've known all my life. I have been told by those who have ridden this train before, that I may also leave everything I've learned up to this point and I will have so much more room to store other stuff, but I will keep the stuff my mother gave me.

I wake up to the sound of bells and the jolting back and forth like some small earthquake. Like a steady rollercoaster with no loops. I am on this train. Of thought. A locomotive with no breaks. This train only stops when it runs out of steam. Thirty minutes later we arrive at Childhood station... as the train slowly rolls to a stop, the heavyset, underdressed, cognac scented conductor tells me that we will be departing shortly. The train will stop here momentarily.

My first stop, my first glimpse at my first hood, childhood. This is the place where kids come to exchange their cap guns for brass knuckles, their marbles for bullets, little girls exchange their barbie dolls and teacups for lip-gloss and tampons. Other kids exchange things that will haunt them forever, things that they did not intend to exchange. Things that were taken from them against their will. Me, all I have to exchange today is my He-man action figure, with battle damage armor, a couple of G.I. Joes, some garbage pal kids' stickers, and a pack of purple bubble yum. I don't know what I want to exchange for. I kind of wanted the guitar, or the book, but I must have come on a busy day, because most of the good shit was gone. I was going to get the playboy magazine and the basketball, but I ended up listening to the homies and I got the same shit as them: the pisto, the frajos, and the spray paint.

This place makes everything look cheap, constrained and colorful. Like an indoor swap meet. As I head towards the boarding area in Childhood Station, two gang recruiters from a particular Barrio were there. These two recruiters from a barrio I refuse to mention cause fuck them putos, were handing out pamphlets and giving a speech of, "Your Barrio needs YOU . . .", type bullshit, with oldies in the background coming from an old rectangle tagged up double deck cassette playing portable boombox that was wrapped with a blue bandana on the handle playing the song, "Hello Stranger" by Barbara Lewis. One of the recruiters, dressed in creased up, oversized black slacks with matching creased up dickie shirt and black and white chucks with bald head and black rectangle sunglasses. He has bad acne craters in his face. Like a young Edward James Olmos must have looked in his early 20's. fuck it, we'll call him Edward James Almost, for now. the other vato was kind of light skinned and no facial hair. He had on some cutoff beige shorts and midway white socks, and you can see he had some hairy ass legs and a scar on his forehead like Harry Potter. Oh shit, that's Harry Patas. I chuckled to myself and Edward James Almost gave me a nasty ass look. We lock our eyes for a second and then I look away. Then he says, "Hey, what chu lookin' at Ese?", I pretend I didn't hear and slowly walk away, and I act like I'm looking for something in my pockets. "Hey Homes, where you from?", he yells, but I don't look back.

In the distance, I could hear the fucken conductor screaming, "ALL ABOARD!". I ran full speed hanging on to my pint-sized clear bottle of Blanco Madero, aka Mata Ratas, my pack of Raleigh smokes and my flat black krylon spray can. I jumped off the childhood station platform in attempts to land on the train through the main door closest to the engine but a force which turned out to be the hand of some extremely strong asshole grabbed me from the back of my t shirt and body-slammed me back onto the platform. "Where 'ya think 'yer goin' bean sprout?" Said this John Cena looking motherfucker in a blue bellboy uniform. He looked like a demented sailor with wild eyes and a Donald duck hat. "You go in the other car son, this here's for VIP's." I looked inside and saw row after row of well dressed, pale-faced passengers. The passengers of this particular side of the train looked like Celene Dion fans going on a field trip to one of her concerts. I picked myself up from the platform and sized up the conductor to see if I can hit him somewhere where he may feel it, but this motherfucker was ripped. Muscles on top of muscles. The type of motherfucker I would have to hit with a bat, or a crowbar and he still may not feel it. My big homey *Pepino* used to say, "There are three types of enemies: the ones you go toe-to-toe with, the type you have to jump with two other homies, and the type you have to put a bullet in their head," This guy was definitely the bullet in the head type. But today, all I did was pick up my stuff, look at his name tag, which had the name *Wilson* written on it, and then I walked away and headed back to the other cart in the back of the train. I returned to my seat and went to sleep.

CHAPTER 2

ARCHNEMESIS

An Equal and Opposite Reaction

My Style Has a Style of Its Own

violin and cello concertos from Rome
underground rap instrumental mementos
Marlboro menthols, pints of merlot

my style has a style of its own
Silvia, Virginia, Maya, and Zora
Gertrude, Selena, Xóchitl and Dora
Anna, Joanna, Wendy, Simone
Sade, Alicia, Rocio, Bjork
It's not me who has acted alone

my style has a style of its own
Initial on belt buckle, black cotton, chrome
Picasso's approach, DaVinci's brushstrokes
Chaka's aerosol spray-can control
Soledad takas, Delano placasos
graffiti in brothels and Carl's Jr restrooms
free hand Insignia Street gang regalia
Tupac and William; Shakurian, Shakespearean
Earvin Johnson magician,
Gretzky Banksy edition
Beastie Boys, Wu Tang, Ludwig van, Wolfgang
Motel 6's, Marriott's, Hilton's
gardens in paradise; lost as John Milton's
slaves' repentance, independence
German shepherds, chihuahuenses
new Americas dependents
wetback witnesses Jehovah's home

my style has a style of its own
Smith and Wesson, Glocks and Colts

nuts and bolts, shocks and volts
peace and harmony's revolts
faders, buttons, and remotes
Pink Floyd, Doors, Ramones and Stones
Guns and Roses, broken bones
broken hearts and broken homes
broken promises galore
like the shit became couture
my style has a style of its own

Titled

Graffitti screams in flat black flair
underneath the freeway overpass
and we stare through the oval glass
normal plans abnormal glands
hormone dance a floral vase
I could never get a portal pass
too informal with my normal ass
Of mortal kombat's, calls of duty, booty calls and halls of beauty
Bluetooth speakers blaring noise
from every teenaged gene-based palm
I may seem human but to all you mutherfuckers on the bus I am alien
I'm on that pencil break, indo shake, 64 Nintendo tape
double dragon
from BMXs to fixies
from fat laces fat farms and fat caps to skinny jeans and Xanax
marijuana jars of purple plastic
adorning the sidewalk like gumby melted in crayoned velvet
the velveteen rabbit that held a mean habit
inhaled the cream mammoth and held like 3 magnets
WTF happened to spelling out what the fuck
damn these iPhones
Smog is evenly distributed between skies over county lines
and hospital scrub blue apartment buildings
Allow me to properly reintroduce myself:
salutations and konichiwa, Habari, ni hao, buna ziua, vitayu,
elsalamo a'lekom, bonjourno, and Buenos Días comrades
Figuratively, I am the grandson of Gertrude Stein
Creator of undefined fine rhyme for the benign blind kind
and the sublime prime mind divine divide refined design
The flying decline of lying denied the dying revived of Rimes remind

Applying behind the grimy kind, define, we dined in live rewind
The lively vine ungodly sign. Anomaly find I'm probably right
Improperly write my property right monopoly ride
Sloppily glide on a novelty night my robbery ripe as a novel rewrite
Tupac Shakurian and Shakespearean, Lynwoodians and Comptonites,
accolades and acolytes, wannabes and look alikes
This is how we categorize and monetize
and super size our super writes
Capitalized, vocalized picturesque conceptualized quantified
revolutionized institutionalized the revised reprised
redesigned and redefined
the top tier and bottom line, the past and future underlined
by the undisputed present time, all behold, the artistic mind

'Lil Enrique Reflects at a House Party

How long shall I let them continue to fuck me?
How long before the sedated monster
awakens from its all too brief slumber?
Do I wish to proceed with this masquerade?
The celebrated sociopath emerges from smoke-filled rooms, red eyed
pumper-nickeled. Jack in the box tacos are dipped in house dressing
and swallowed by the young spectators
with cotton candy-scented vapes
and baby pink Versace sweatpants.
How do I get talked into these gatherings
of premeditated fuckery and loud perfumes.
The not-so-special Olympics of educated haters
and overrated orators exists.
I am the pouting piranha
who lusts over electric eels and poisonous jellyfish.

Going toe to toe with conceited concubines
much too philandering to be a philanthropist.
The arcane Jacko lantern
dressed in freshly ironed pedal pushers and overpriced blouses.
As they march nonchalantly down the fuck boy parade.
They quietly construct the cleverest hashtags their mind could muster.
They bump the latest assortment
of the days whack rap on their overpriced iPhones.
I suddenly returned to a drag of my cigarette and ashed it outwardly
toward the high pitch hackles and snobby remarks.
I rejoice within the cozy confines of
the suddenly premiered, so sweet, cherry-filled truth:
they can't fuck with me here.

Gangster Chicks

Back in the day, I used to kick it with gangster chicks,
Like Casper: powder skinned, blonde, dark lip liner on.
Blue Ben Davis pants on, creased, charcoal gray Frisco Bens shirt,
Black and white British knights shoes.
Hairspray, moose, blue tattoos.
We used to kiss against the chain link fence
in dusty alleys under mutant lemon trees.
She was a sloppy kisser whose breath tasted of
Spearmint bubble gum and menthol cigarettes.
Piney and numbingly fresh.
Like kissing a bottle of vaporub with lips.
Her forehead barely reached my chin.
Our lips remained smacking intertwined.
I occasionally peeked and looked about,
Then returned to the darkness of her kisses.
After 30 minutes of saliva swapping,
We would hold hands and walk with no destination.
Wiping lipliner from my face.
Small talk was too tiny to recall.
It was time for her to go.
Back to her friend's house
Where her parents thought she was supposed to be.
Sleepover lies.
I would walk her to her friend's house,
And watched her disappear thru the side window
And into her friend's bedroom.
And I would never see her again.
Like Mousy.
Another gangster chick, but older.
Feathered blonde hair, mascara'd eyelashes

Like black whips that swung each time she batted them.
Spaghetti string tops, bronze skinned shoulders,
Nipples protruded and nearly peeked from her blouse.
A single-mother who smoked and cursed.
And always paid in cash for 2-hour motel rooms.
Stab wounds on her lower back.
Puffy caterpillar stitched skin mementos
Given to her by her enemies.
Forget me nots.
We interlocked fingers
And kissed, playing chewing gum volleyball with our tongues.
Until the gum became a tasteless puddy pulp.
Cognac and cocaine diet to preserve a girlish figure.
She ain't so gangster in the nude, moaning.
Slim bronze hands, burgundy colored nails
Throw gang signs out the car window.
2 Puffy gangster girls dressed like male thugs
In raider jerseys throw gang signs back.
"Pull over" she says to me while looking at the sideview mirror.
I obey.
"What's up bitch!" she yells
her arms towards heaven.
Green Flathead Screwdriver in hand.
Smoking a joint.
Eyes half-shut, reeking of Remy Martin and bitter cough medicine.
"Fuck these scary ass bitches," she says,
As she sits and closes the door.
"Let's go."
We proceed to her home
Where I drop her off and never see her again.

Like Glossy,

A cute young chick from South Central.

She loved to sing.

We did a song together before my homey started to cockblock.

I really wanted to hang out with her,

But,

She died in a burning car crash during a police chase.

The officers could not undo her seatbelt in time.

And she died engulfed in flames.

The driver lived.

Sometimes, I remember.

When I used to hang out

With gangster chicks.

Meduso

Look at this
Look at this onlookers,
Look.
Looking good, good looking!
Taste it, it taste,
And look like a look-alike.

Onomatopoeia.
We are lyricists
Are we
Not lyricists?
If not
Then what
Are we?

Ponds I ponder
Pounds of wonder.
Wonder fo' sounds
Sounds of red now.
Retina. I speak
Enigmas to souls
With gang related
Sacraments. All water
Is holy.

From the vantage
Point we peak at
All we capture
Is captivity.

God, if I kiss
The corn plants
Before they flower
Will they know
Me postmortem?

Fear less, fear some,
I fear not.
No Fear.

Let me braid
Your snakes
Medusa.

Don't Forget to Take Your Meds

Run when you see me
call when you need me
never mind who broke you
I am here to help rebuild
to refill the dreams they spilled from you
the unfulfilled goals killed
who I am is not important,
we shall cross paths again
and you won't recognize me
but today I am your savior

I am here to elevate you
and to love you when they hate you
I am here just to remind you
to give sight to those who blind you
to refine you...
to assign you one task
to help you wave goodbye to your past
so sit back relax
chill
may I reveal the "you" concealed?
I am here to assure you that yes God is yours...
...love is yours and you are worthy...
pay no attention to these burdens
I have brought you reassurance
that though burdens will continue
salvation is within you
and you are right where you belong
we were meant to tread along
this path whose wrath
has made us strong

So today I've come with strength
because tomorrow I may be the one who needs you
it's been a pleasure not to meet you
but to serve you, nonetheless
now I leave you well refreshed
don't forget to take your meds

Disappointment

Back to gutters in a hurry
Goddess remains her title
but back she goes to those...
ungrateful foes. Distasteful hoes.
There she is, in front of me.
Carefully placing the glass tip
upon her puckered mouth...
like ceramic trombones that gurgle smoke and water.
Her tone has changed,
and who am I?
The guy hitting a joint.
I came to disappoint.

Self-Development

I am a negative picture in a dark room.
Developing in darkness.
It is ironic how, in darkness,
we bring things to light.
No aid. No help.
Developing myself.
Self-portrait. Selfie.
Like pictures, every day I develop more.
Images become clearer as the negative remains in darkness.
Forever printed, the negative of me.
But without it, how positive could I see?
Or could I be?
In order to find and appreciate the positive,
one must first develop the negative.
Therefore, self-development begins—
in a dark room.

Inspiration's Return

After years without her presence,
she has finally returned. Is it really her?
Is inspiration here?
A ghost with no mass,
no shape, no fear.
Yet I know when she is here.
I feel more sincere,
so deep yet so clear,
when she is near
I get sort of cocky, it's weird,
like nothing can stop me,
nor time, nor space,
nor man, no one, no way...
She is here,
like a kid who hasn't seen mom in a year.
I feel her, a woman who longs to appear.
She has returned,
my insides are starting to burn
then I start seeing letters wherever I turn.
Her mundane return, I can't wait to rush her.
For 26 months I've been wanting to touch her.
Wanting; righteously, and when we touch,
our touch is such that everybody feels it too.
I wonder if she grew
and what type of situations she's been through
since the last time she was here.
Man, I sound like a teenager
in love for the first time.
Let me just chill and try to get back to sleep.
It is 3:23 AM and I can't sleep.
I'm up... waiting for inspiration and
she's just arrived.

They Need Heroes 2

"I be fucking up huh, Low-key,"
that's what he said to me
I smiled back free, while tree debris—
getting tatted by me
just take the pain man
it'll be over before you're sober
and if it's not, take another shot
that will hit the spot
a black handle of an automatic handgun—
peeks out the pocket of his blue 501 jeans
like a baby kangaroo—
hanging from his mother's pouch
there he stands, shirtless
asking me to tell him again
about Paradise Lost
intrigued by Satan's point of view
he peeps game, like a camouflaged hunter—
with a duck whistle
here are we, present day Long Beach
and I am discussing British literature—
with active gang members and fugitives
He's trying to correlate the lives of John Milton
Tupac Shakur, and the effect of writers on society
political, economic and psychological influences
of writers, poets, and artists
Remy Martin cascades over ice rocks
on crystal blue glasses
his thin body: a skin chalkboard—
for tattoo artists
with homemade tattoo machines

powered by 2 D size batteries,
and held together with black electric tape
looking at the ink letters, brings back—
blood mixed with
Indian ink-scented memories
of smoke filled rooms, Bacardi bottles,
and using eyes as pick-up lines
seducing goddesses in parking lots
a modern day Midas
all I touch becomes graffiti
and corroborates my presence
the complexity of inner-city life is
simply simplicity
poverty is freedom stagnant
incarceration is conditional slavery
and we seem in between nature and machine
the embryonic, undeveloped fetus of our dreams
nothing good flourishes from bad streets
he extends both hands with tattooed knuckles
and begins to explain his thesis:
"On one side, you got scumbags, losers, rapists, thieves
and on the other side, you got police
but I don't fit in either one of these"
he contends, with half opened eyes
and small lazy smile
"I'm somewhere in between,"
he says, he is the police of thieves
things ain't always what it seems
you may think gunshots in vain
when in fact maintain the peace

preserve balance to this environment
by all means, I continue talking reads
such as Richard II, Hamlet
and Sylvia Plath, Canterbury Tales
while hollow point shells and 2nd hand smoke prevails
literature wins where incarceration and probation fails
just parts of entries and documentaries
of hood experiments and studies
I'm studying villains
they need heroes too

Early Morning Strolling

Not knowing where I'm going
the moon is still above me
the sidewalk seems to hug me
as if the streets do love me
the good the bad the ugly
the hood the straps the money
the food attracts the hungry
the dirty stacks of laundry
graffiti on the palm tree
as prostitutes stroll softly
like a funeral procession
and though we've never met
we both share the same depression
the same mirrors we have stared at
paint a dissimilar reflection
But the streets do love me
they see beyond perception
they seek no explanation
don't believe in expectations
they see me strolling early morning
not knowing where I'm going
and they just let me be
the streets have faith in me

Mega Millions 2.7

As an English major, I never cared for mathematics, vice versa. But today, I want to speak on a very particular and very revolutionary form of mathematics that perhaps has swelled in the tip of your tongue momentarily, but once rationale kicked in, you decided to swallow it as I have many of times. Well today is not the day. Today I will speak a new form of mathematics to the world that no ear has ever heard. I've come today to speak to you about the simplicity of the most complex number in mathematics today. #27. This is Californian mathematics. What is 10 + 3? 13 add one to that number and it equals 14 13 and 14 13 and 14 13 and 14 13 and 14 I'm here to talk to you about the number 27. Potentially, the most powerful number in the state of California. And possibly the country and maybe the world. This is an introduction of the idea of metric advancement in civil engineering. I am not a mathematician but the most powerful number in California is the number 27.

I'm Leaving Los Angeles

I'm leaving the city of Los Angeles
her yellowish fingers of dry palm trees on the side of the 5-freeway
wave goodbye to me
the overpass screams at me in colorful graffiti accents
as the traffic and the smog sluggishly dissipate behind me
the hands of Los Angeles gently let me go
and my eyes feel the texture of its scattered architecture
for just one last time, she bids me goodbye
with its weeping, willow leaves
and eucalyptus trees
in the midst of its hills
from her green spring shoulders, she lets me go
like slow, lateral raindrops parting from her soul
as we waltz in her traffic jam one last time
at a distance: her sunny, concrete hands
a soft smile escapes me
I will return soon
I wipe tepid tears from her aqueduct eyes
and bid my goodbyes, to my city, Los Angeles

The Bipolar Express: Act 2

(Ten years later)

"Levantese pinche morro!" yelled the heavyset, underdressed cognac-scented conductor, while lifting the orange foamed headphones from my head with his dark brown baton. I rub my eyes and stretch my arms slowly while yawning at the same time. Wow, it's been like a ten year dream up to this point. My body had changed, my face had changed. I had four tattoos and three new scars. I now smoked cigarettes and weed and drank hard liquor every now and then. Unfortunately, I was still a virgin. I was also now a member of a tagging crew notorious for vandalizing city property, breaking into cars, and doing lots of graffiti. My crew went from being taggers to tag bangers. And even though we were mostly high school and middle school kids, our crew, like many others, would be given an ultimatum by the powers that be. We were told we had to either join a gang or dismantle our tag-banging bullshit. But being kids, we did neither one of these things. This would put us in a fucked situation in which granted all the gangs in our vicinity "The Go Ahead" and encouraged the assaulting and abolishment of our forbidden little group.

Clearly, by some means, I survived the green light era, and I was ready to put it all behind me. But this would not be as easy as it sounded. At this point I also started writing poetry and my world would begin to get complicated. I figured, at my next stop, I could drop off all this drama I had gotten into and simply trade it in for a new car, a babe, and a nice career.

It is daytime. Out the window one can see unfamiliar, endless fields with rows of plowed brown dirt and scattered, dusty farmworkers with dusted white rags or bandanas over their mouths and dirty baseball caps or tattered straw hats on their profusely sweating heads. They bend their bodies under the unforgiving sun and move like injured robots, snatching tomatoes up and tossing them into the conveyer-belt of this orange machine the size of a house, where many female farm workers stand wearing rubber gloves assembling boxes and filling them up with red juicy tomatoes as hard as apples and the size of a standard sized softball.

Coming up is my next stop, adulthood station. This is the place where I will try to drop off some of the shit I've picked up along the way along with some of the other shit I picked up from childhood. As the train slowly rolls to a complete stop all the youngsters hop out and make their way into adulthood. I'm ready to trade-in all this bullshit drama and the spray can too. I think I will keep the weed, cigarettes and pisto though. This place is filled with beautiful vibrant art. There is a bronze statue of Pancho Villa on a horse. Also, Cantinflas murals and a blood-in blood-out mural, you know the one in the riverbed with Miclo, Cruzito, and Paco, that one. There is one gigantic mural about three stories high and about a basketball court size across which is my favorite. It is titled, "Reynas" and is a beautiful piece done by Siqueiros' Grandson, Ramonsito "Poncho" Siqueiros, that pays homage to the Latinas Reynas of the Americas consisting of a poker table with the following characters sitting at this table playing poker. From left to right; La India María, Jenny Rivera, Lola Beltrán, Selena, Frida Kahlo, Dolores Huerta, La Virgen De Guadalupe, Celia Cruz, Sor Juana Inés de la Cruz, Sno the Product, Linda Ronsdant, Ellen Ochoa, and Evita Peron.

As I step into the main shop, I can see kids coming out with mustaches on their faces, goatees, with girls on their arms and construction helmets on their heads. Fuck, not again, they don't have shit left. "Sorry guys, we are all out of careers until next week," said a loud chubby and short white guy whose voice resembled Joe Pesci. In the corner of my eye I spotted four gang recruiters handing out pamphlets and signing up kids and jumping them into their hood. "Hey, what's up little homies, how would you like to start on an exciting new career path guaranteed to keep you on the edge of your seat, high as fuck, and fucking with a new haina every week?" It was motherfucking Edward James Almost, listening to "Between the Sheets" by the Isley Brothers, saying, "Your new criminal career awaits." Harry Patas is there too, and he spotted me. "Hey, check it out ese, ain't that the little leva from the childhood station?" I continued walking and went into the adult-hood trade shop. I hurried up and traded all my childhood bullshit and told the shopkeeper to give me whatever they had in exchange. Then I grabbed the bag and quickly walked out the back door as the two gang recruiters, Harry Patas and Edward James Almost, walk in the shop looking for me.

As I'm walking towards the train platform from the back of the store, the adult hood mentality started getting into my psyche and I suddenly stop walking and rudely interrupt my smooth ass getaway and think, "Fuck these putos! Why am I running like a little bitch?" All these motherfuckers from barrios been punking us taggers for years and beating us up, robbing us, and killing us. Only a few motherfuckers I know that actually stood up against these bastards. I'm tired of running from these fools. Today I'm going to confront them, and they are either going to kick my ass or I'm going to kick theirs. With an air of arrogance and lunacy, heart beating like a machine gun on new year's eve, I walk breathing heavy, feeling the nerves on my shoulders tense up, popping my knuckles, fists trembling like a volcano before it blows, teeth clinched, 100 monarch butterflies with razor blade wings shredding at the walls of my stomach. The high pitch yell of 3 thousand years' worth of ancestral lineage enters my heart and beat faster, and faster. The war drums of a conquered civilization rising up to its oppressor, swimming out of boiling pools of blood. The culmination of all the foul acts committed against my people have gathered up as energy and charged up the battery that is me. The empty vessel at sea with no meaning has finally reached its course. As my fists have ceased to exist and instead a battalion of bronze skinned phantasms on horseback takes their place and I am the general in command who yelled CHARGE at the top of my lungs. As I head towards the front entrance of the shop and before I got to the door, Edward James is walking out talking to Harry, who is walking behind him and before this motherfucker sees me I throw a right cross with all my might, right to his skinny ass chest, BOOOOM!, he ran right into it. He falls to the ground and starts shaking with his hands balled up and folded inward and twisted, in an epileptic seizure. His homeboy Harry Patas looks at me with the eyes of a starving dog looking at another dog who is trying to snatch the last piece of meat off his lonesome plate. His homey is his main concern now and drops down trying to help him, but I had not had my fill of mayhem. I needed more blood to quench this monster that raged inside me for years, begging me to let him out and play or one day, he would say, he was going to bust out and manifest his terror upon the unsuspecting earth. And that is exactly what he did. I aimed my rage at Harry Patas who was tending to his homeboy Edward. I took this opportunity to throw a left uppercut directly at the chin of Harry Patas. You heard his top and bottom teeth collide with one another like a cow bell when I followed with a straight

60

right to his cheek bone, and he was down on his back. "That's the last time you putos fuck with me!" I assured Harry Patas, by this time Edward had stopped convulsing but the way I was feeling I did not give a fuck if Edward made it or not. All I knew is I had killed before and I could do it once again if I had to. Bird embryos or humans are all the same shit to me, I told myself. the realization of what I've done had not yet sank in. but I had just made some powerful and treacherous enemies. Right now, there was no consciousness of consequence. Right now, it was a celebration of the damaged ego of the underdog. This was a very strange victory. One that is rarely witnessed and even less commemorated. But I celebrated with myself. I knew what just happened. I was in a fucked situation where the odds were firmly against me, and I took a shot and was triumphant. I stood there momentarily, fists still shaking, breathing heavily like I just finished running a mile around a high school football field. People started gathering and giving me props. Harry Patas stood up and helped Edward James Almost to his feet as two more recruiters came running in the distance. I came back to my senses. All I could think of is to run. But I couldn't run. I waited til the other two came. I tried to do the same to them, but I couldn't. They beat my ass. Harry Patas joined his two friends and unleashed a vengeful counter assault on my face and stomach. His attempts did not face me though, I felt numb and covered my face as best as I could as the kicks from dirty Nike Cortez and chucks continued. Edward James Almost stands on the side like a pissed off coach shouting, "Stomp that Puto!", with the team spirit of Pat Riley at a playoff game.

"Hey, leave him alone, I already called the cops", yells one of the shop owners. "Fuck you bitch!" yells Harry Patas. "Let's go home," says Edward James Almost before walking up to me and kicking me on my back creating a thump sound that echoed in my chest and caused me to throw up on myself. His last goodbye was spitting on my bleeding ear. At this point I can't hear anything anymore. All I see is Edward James Almost hurrying away with his homeboys turning his hand into a pistol and aiming it at me. I couldn't hear anything, but I read his lips going, "Bang, Bang." I tried to get up . . . but everything went blank.

CHAPTER 3

UNSCRUPULOUS MOTIVES

Purpose for Your Service

Forgive

With the confidence of gods, we dare show our faces
upon the hordes of conflicting continents and
constant constellations of content content with conflict.
Concaved context, contextual contest of countless complex
camaraderie's conquest.
Decomposing compositions composed
and poised as poisonous posies posing.
Composing as composts in campos encompass
excommunicated husbands that remain great parents
to otherwise undermined childlike beings of divine texture.

One sees best with no vision
when lids, like purple curtains, fall upon stages of darkness.
Small sparks magnifying illuminate features
familial creatures from poor righteous teachers
enlightened the frightened.
Tongue kissing titties of Titan
no being frightened
only the end of fright: fright-end
let us not believe. be-leave: a fuck word.
Instead of be-leaving, let us know.
For belief requires trust and faith and hope.
I'd rather know who the fuck tore a page off my notebook
and what ever happened to Hendy Foot.

A Poet named Ronnie came to Vista Continuation School in Lynwood.
A sister from another mister
who came to claim one of her own brother from another mother.
She would discover me by accident and not intended
like North American Indies;
I vetoed his-story books.

Embargoes of plagiarized creative nonfiction
fixations of fuckerish balderdash.
Audacious bastards!
They sell us cake and help us eat it too.

But regardless, bike horns on grocery carts become corporate.
There is no need to mistreat street vendors,
but there is no reason not to forgive those who mistreat.
Let us patch these rips between us.
Even geniuses fuck up, but in this class,
everyone's entitled to a second chance,
a second glance, love at third sight.
The one thing we have in common is our differences.
We have common differences and the confidence of gods.
Forgive.

Past

Why are you alive and I'm dead,
when we both have the same bullshit in our head?
Why the fuck am I dead and not you,
when you know that I am a way better father than you?
Why didn't death come get you instead?
Because truth be told you're the reason why I'm dead.
Why did I have to die and not you?
I'm only here because of the drugs you introduced me to.
Why must my son grow up without a dad?
It should have been your bastarded son eternally sad.
Why does my girl have to be without her man,
when you treated like shit every woman that you've had?
I know why you're alive and I'm dead,
because you still have to pay for all the bullshit you did.

Axe It Dental

With Conditions One is never absolutely Free. I Am Free.
Therefore, this will be a poem depending on who reads it.
It will attempt to not be classified as formal nor free verse.
But please, feel free to judge or categorize it, or stereotype it.
This poem will at times not identify as a poem.
In certain settings,
it will hide disguised as a lesson in someone's online classroom.
This poem will be the neo of writings.
It will be The Ultimate Warrior of its class.
Sometimes, when you think it is a conversation,
this poem will Lowkey feel poetic.
No one can mistake this poem for a song, a sonnet, or a villanelle,
no, this poem will be able to attend various functions as dialogue,
or as a reflection or even as a letter of complaint.
This poem will intentionally attempt to avoid its structure, meter.
It will try to not show its rhyme scheme
or its ability to present imagery
nor will it allude to personification,
nor will it be an ode.
It will be too short to be an epic and too long to be a tanka.
This poem will have no pronouns,
but feel free to segregate it into a category or a genre.
This poem can be considered art or not.
This poem is in no way connected to other poems.
This poem has no expectations of ever being printed, read,
or of being part of a collection of poetry.
This poem, though it is not prejudice, it does not identify as a poem
or as a work of some artist's catalog.

This poem is self-assured,
it has no trust issues and
has no alternative motives or agendas.
This poem was not planned but has been inspired,
it is not structured but it is constructed,
it is not poetic, but it is metaphoric,
it is not rhythmic but melodic.
This poem is not inspirational, but it has self-esteem.
It is not self-centered, but it is not insecure.
Feel free to let this poem make you feel empowered or weak.
Use it like a drug if you will
and discard it like a napkin when it no longer serves its purpose.
This writing has no destination in mind.
It is not free verse nor is it a ballad.
If anything, this poem is what the title suggests it is:
an accidental poem.

Writs-Ardry

There is no definite definition
for his missionary mission.
Dictionaries burn in shame
for lacking the substantiation.
The proof that may bring truth
and conviction to his diction.
A false depiction is crude detection.
Written pessimistic, masochistic crucifixion.
The wordsmith's rubrics are cubic Rubik's
a cubist's blueprints linguistic Supplex.
Genain quadruplets acoustic movements,
a lucid nuisance on Wordsworth's footsteps is he...
In the world of word wizardry,
his position is the
archbishop of harsh diction
as Henry Kissinger of carefree literature,
his reflexes are remixes
of Felix the Cat and Heathcliff's
Spanglish and broken English eclipses
an urban version of a Merman virgin
who operates like a nervous surgeon
haiku typhoons brain wave tsunamis
and word quakes
tongue twist tornadoes and vocab volcanoes
English sonnets are dwindling comets
he'll bitch slap grammar with his witchcraft phonics.

The wizardry of magic words:
the ways where waving wands would work
whence winds which wail will whelm with woe
why wonder why we worship war
when wolves with white wool wean to wound,
We wit woo wonder woman's womb
and wait invisibly to burn the witchery.
While wantons wroth,
we wrought word wizardry.

Present

What is the color of your mood tonight?
What may I soothe you with,
reboot you with.
Libraries of words I have for you.
Letters you need to scoop.
And blow this alphabet soup,
because it burns when you swallow it.
You, first born this side of El Paso.
The kangol tassel,
child of a tangled castle.
Asphalt Prince, I know you
must deal with these asshole pricks,
but I will be there to witness your dad's old pics.
See the flash but never say cheese.
Cursed with words forever say please.
Like wars are cursed to forever say peace.

I know you are the type to be in solitude alone
by yourself and if you happen to burp you say excuse me.
I'm proud of you.
At times you have been mother and father,
even to children unfathered by you.
Allow me to curtsy till it hurts me.
Please receive these depleted flowers of mine,
a colloquial bouquet of words.
But receive them.
Make room so they sit next to you,
and feed them.
Need them and leave them
as soon as you greet them.

Conversations till dawn.

Ounces of any chemical that you're on.

Mowing your lawn, I wish I could love you less.

Let us hear your compositions till I know them by heart.

Let us marvel at your genius.

Let us carpool watching *Minions*.

Let's appreciate the hideous.

Let me taste your ugly truths.

Salads from these rotten fruits.

Let me produce smiles from you as if God was watching softly from atop abandoned buildings.

Let us smile 'til we are cheek boned.

Let us freestyle rap to ringtones.

Happiest birthday,

from the grave I wish you orchids.

Mighty morphins your endorphins never orphaned.

End of torment sadness dormant.

At the grandiose performance.

We have come to pay respects

with coronas and Gillette's,

gang initiation memories,

fellow followers of felonies.

May the mulch demote thy enemies.

In the melted heat of snow,

I shall never let you go.

These and other sacred things
I need but never hear from you.

The Lost and Found

Part 1

Sometimes, poetry hides from me craftly, she hides for seasons, sometimes, I find myself seeking, wanting, longing, missing. What a lovely inconvenience it is to miss, the absence of her is a beautiful tragedy, missing curves and lines for tongue twisting rhymes. To miss is to retain someone or something in their absence. Sometimes, poetry hides from me effectively, she hides for seasons at times. Sometimes, poetry hides from me, sometimes, poetry finds me.

Part 2

I find myself scouting, tracking, searching, hunting. What a desperate, lovely thought it is to stalk. Without her, every month is a crippled walk in the park, the blind, blindfolded scavenger hunt in the dark. Remembering style and verse, her lip licking words. To remember, it is to hold someone or something long after they are gone. Sometimes, poetry hides from me, sometimes, poetry finds me.

Seven Syllable Sonnet

Greetings from across the seas
readings from the loss of peace
city full of Boston teas
pity full less Constantine's

Beautiful as constant dreams
uniform is tossed in streams
funerals as dark as beams
universal law's extremes

Poems, of a nonsense, scream
poets that are on this screen
no this ain't a thoughtless stream
love is in a box this eve.

This new form is Antoinette
seven syllable sonnet.

Building Books

First, reduce the use of fuels seek all alternatives to power.
Never stop until success, soft micro office 2013 preferred.
First, page layout, on size enter, six-by-nine and then margins 0.5.
Then we insert shapes and pictures, cover page.
And then a title page, blank page.
Then the third insert, subtitle, then a blank and then the credits
Then the main title, then the preface, then the table, then the intro,
then acknowledgements, skip one page
and begin always on the right or odd side of an open book.
Insert, header, add page number, choose your font
after last page, 10-line bio about the author, then back page,
blurb, and go find a sponsor.
Then choose your binding. And choose your paper.
Hard or soft cover. Then choose your ink,
then your size (6x9) in color or black and white.
(We skipped the most important thing; must add content in between
and if the content of your book happens to be
how to build a book of blueprints
then refer back to the first step and keep following my footsteps.)

Forthwith

No matter if the worst in man jump up from them as monsters do
when debris of beaten ghosts plunge from broken worlds above
even when they spring their cleverly positioned traps beneath you
and the grainy drops of terror start to fill you; please continue.

When servant beasts grow displeased from being made the fool
and blitz you for they texture you not fit enough to rule
when predatory instincts are silenced by the horde
if to halt is what they bid you, remember to continue.

Once totality has failed and the nil becomes an option
and futile pediments to deities who forever fail to hear you
come tumbling back to you from the darkened blue of space
and hesitate your state of grace, do not retrace continue.

When falling stars illuminate your night with blinding splendor
and brand the earth with fractures reaching far beyond its center
and everything you knew of faith for man has slowly vanished
when hopelessness is all that lies within you still continue.

Though earthquakes and tsunamis be the fate of fellow man
and evolution threatened by the hands of Mother Nature;
if love, you once possessed, became the evil that prevails
and merrie worlds of revenue offend you, just continue.

Though daggers may slice at you from the thick of ghastly mist
the silky musk of bloody drips; the red that warms your lips
when all attack your helpless back with words that rupture souls,
if any life at all remains within you, do continue.

When evil men surround you with intent to break your faith
and wicked clever women twist your loving words to hate
and origami figures of your soul is all that's left
if death herself shall halt you and forbid you, do continue.

When alabaster figures have been placed in all your temples
and statues of your gods have been torn from under earth
and desecrated graves is what's left of all your elders
if all the things you are, they now forbid you, do continue.

When the bulk of all your enemies have gathered up at once
with intent to shoot their blades on you and stab you with their guns;
when they keep from you their bitches and they sick on you their sons;
if fangs break skin, injecting venom in you, still continue.

When the grimy grimly hands of grim reapers reach about you
and death's touch has clutched flush on the lush that is you're being;
when the wooden curtain closes, and they shovel you with roses
wonder if you will be parched or have it in you to continue.
P.X

Delusions of the Ethnocentric

Take up the hue man's burden
send forth the best ye breed
unbind your sons from slavery
and heed their master's creed
with weight from heavy burden
has fluttered folk and child
the heart that fed the people
from feeble hands of vile

take up the hue man burden
impatient Hue's reprise
unveil the face of terror
and dive into its eyes
by broken speech and temple
unbounded times made gain
to reap his brother's pocket
and profit from his pain

take up the hue man's burden
the gentle peace of war
fulfill the mouths with famine
and bid them back for more
and when your goal is nearest
the ends of others fought
you're foolish heathens' folly
supplanted hope for aught

take up the hue man's burden
the gaudy rule of kings
that views the turf and beings
as sundry common things

the doors you shall not enter
no borders shall ye cross
rebuke me solemn splendor
for arrowed albatross

take up the hue man's burden
and seek his old remorse
the love from those he hated
have aided those ye forced
the cry of ghosts ye murdered
ah slowly toward the light
who brought us free from bondage
our loved Egyptian night

take up the hue man's burden
and bear ye food for less
liberty and freedom
are teal in hue and dress
and all who cry and whisper
from all ye failed to do
thy weight from heavy burden
ye self hath wroth on you

take up the hue man's burden
be gone from wildly craze
the weighty thorny crown
the harsh resentful ways
comes now to check your manhood
for all your thankless years
to taw your dear-bought system
with judgment of your peers

take up the hue man's burden
embark it if you dare
no wisdom is existent
to aid the ill prepared

take up the hue man's burden
and find there's nothing there
delusions of a cross
you thought ye been cursed to bear,
burden is the hue of man
the only thing we humans share.

Written by Carlos Ornelas on Sunday March 18, 2012, 1:42 AM, Long Beach. CA at the sanctuary. A late rebuttal to the poem titled "The White Man's Burden" written by the great poet Rudyard Kipling, 1899

Dedicated to none and to all.
Just another spontaneous overflow.
Art for art's sake.

Shero

I commiserate with murderers and invaders because I am human.
I benefit from trails of tears, and mass murders of indigenous peoples.
How do I benefit?
I am American. Not in America though, only abroad.
I had to be poet.
Heroes never invited me to Sadie Hawkins.
I am villainy's symbol, proudly.
Gold Medusa head pendant decapitated.
Malevolence, petunias, ursulas, cruellas,
I've got a posse of medusas...
They turned me to stone.
One poem.
One look.
Melt my ice,
snake eyes...
The head is full of king cobras.
Adopted a martyr and fathered an orphan child.
I close my eyes and they all vanish...
Have you ever dreamt in Spanish?
I am Shang Tsung of archetypes,
male mystique.
Poet.
Too wizard to be magician.
The stereo, arche, and proto type...
Man femme fatale
I am,
hero to villains.

Future

Daddy Daddy why are we so far apart,
separated by the weekdays?

Why does mommy have another,
why am I to call him father,
why can't you just live with us?
"Minecraft, YouTube, make me blind.
Come and occupy my time".

Daddy, I don't understand.
Mommy loves another man?

Daddy, Daddy, hold my hand.
Does it hurt to be a man?
Have you swallowed all you can?
Where's my footprints in the sand?

Daddy, talk like Patrick Star,
Make me laugh until I barf.
Let's pretend we'll never part.
Let's pretend we have no heart.
Let us cry only through art.

Dad, oh Daddy,
Can we play,
Before childhood goes away?
Before Mother makes us move,
Into condos with no view.
Into condos... with no you.

Let us watch another movie
while you bake us something grand.
Let me memorize tattoos
that have faded from your hand.

Let me memorize your eyes
just in case they separate us.
Is this force that guides our course
also from the God that made us?

I won't cry Dad, I'll be a big boy,
Just like you told me to be.
Don't cry Daddy, be a big boy,
be a big boy just like me.

Tired

sorry if I do not write like you
but you must understand
I didn't know English until the 6th grade
I learned it among six graders
who were sexually active and gang-related
I apologize for my lack of campfire memories
and for not bonding with grandparents
I truly do regret not being able to share the good old days
for my old days carry the stench of burnt buildings and dirt weed
my memoirs contain moments of embarrassment
from standing in county lines at middle school cafeterias
wearing yardsale hand-me-down garments
please pardon if my speech resembles rap
please forgive me if I seem antisocial but
I've gone through
episodes,
betrayals,
suicide attempts,
incarcerations,
withdrawals,
near death experiences,
gunfights at baptism parties,
false accusations,
poverty,
and homelessness
that makes it difficult
to find common things to talk about
Please pardon me if I don't take time anymore
to write about the perfect love
but my love was never perfect

no love is perfect,
a love that's worth it
a love that came in the form of pain,
with $10 to your name,
and calling in surveys on receipts
to get a, "buy-one get-one free" coupon code for Jumbo Jacks
Forgive me if I don't write sweet cheery shit
to soothe your palate but
I've been busy, somewhat dizzy,
trying to figure out why this fucking car won't start
And why pride does not reside where Spanish speaking workers hide
on18-wheeled casket rides, across the El Paso border
I'm sorry if I don't write right
But it's my right to write with a fire's appetite
I don't worry if it's right, I just write
I just write
I don't apologize for doing what I was born to do
But if my words offended you,
my apologies

The Bipolar Express: Act 3

I woke up, and 28 years had passed by. I was still at this station. But it was nighttime. The station was empty, and not a train in sight. Man, I can't believe I missed the train. I still had my bag I had traded in the adulthood trade shop. I never knew what I traded for. Holy shit, I barely fit into my clothes. I must have gained 50 pounds. I had more tattoos and more scars. And I now made a wheezing sound when I breathe. There is a limp on my leg, and I smell like I haven't showered in weeks. I am now homeless.

I look inside my bag. To my surprise, I find the stem of a glass pipe burnt black, a piece of burnt foil, a straw cut in half, a green king lighter, a used syringe, a small bottle of Taka Vodka half ways gone, a losing $2 dollar scratcher, and a small photo album. Is this what I had traded my childhood for?

I felt like such a fool. My life had passed me as I slept away for years. I had done and accomplished nothing good in my life. I was a homeless addict and a drunk with nothing to show for it. As I think back, I never had an adolescence. I went from childhood and straight into adulthood. As I left the adulthood train station, I suddenly realized, there was no fucking train. There was no station. I was at the MTA metro station on Long Beach and PCH. All this time I had just imagined this whole scenario. I was insane. And I was out of my medication. Roaming through the streets of Downtown Long Beach with the rest of the walking dead. The tears in my eyes began to blur my vision as I tried to accept this new founded truth.

I am walking alongside the platform and in the distance I see the light of the first train of the day heading towards me with bells slightly ringing. I knew then and there I was not going to accept this truth and decided that I would meet my end in the tracks of this metro train. I started to empty out all the shit in my bag and found a piece of a cigarette and grabbed one of the lighters and lit it up.

As the train approached closer, I was planning my doom. I threw the contents of the bag on the floor and threw the bag also. As I look closer, the photo album opens up and I see a picture of me with a little girl smiling next to me and a baby boy in my arms. It looks like we are at a kid's party. The train is now about a block away and getting closer, and closer.

CHAPTER 4

ANTIHERO

I was made by the struggle
my first struggle began before I was one.
Actually, before birth: when my struggle begun.
I was conceived during struggle so heavenly sweet
the result of a troubled couples marriage retreat.
One weekend of peace; and a lifetime of war.
Adversities child in premature form.

The Poor Rich

The poor.
We gather up in packs because it's cold.
Appreciating everything.
Our children are of gold.
Efficiency is everything.
And everyone is bold.
To live in such conditions.
It's a mission to be old.
Since most will die before their 24th.
Deprived of needed things we can't afford.
And for the rich, all things are in accord.
Our prayers haven't reached to heaven's door.
Or are our prayers for a different Lord?
Or is it 'cause we never needed more?
Believe in peace since every day is war.
That's why the richest people are the poor.

When Villains Need Heroes

when villains get drowsy in back of classrooms
heroes have picnics on slow cloudy Mondays
when villains are busy avoiding their doom
heroes walk barefoot on sandy blonde beaches
while villains are sought for countless of felonies
heroes repose within secret identities
while heroes gain glory and marshal parades
villains stay hidden with freedom forbidden
saying to themselves, "the world is a villain"

Yo Nephew

True, it's a free country, but check this out.

Be careful what you choose to be.

Hey. Listen to me, attentively please.

Be careful what you choose to be.

When people say, "It's easy to pull the trigger. Anyone can pull a trigger," that is bullshit.

Not just anyone can pull a trigger; that shit takes heart. That doesn't mean you should rely on guns. You must handle your shit, naked if you have to. With no aid from guns, knives, or none of that shit. Guns are to be used only as a last resort.

But if you got the heart, to pull a trigger, and not in the shooting range anyone can do that shit. I'm talking about busting in public type shit. If you have the heart to do shit like that, on the street, imagine what you can do out there, in the world.

I'm not talking about gangbanging or pulling triggers. I'm talking about pushing buttons, not pulling triggers, but pulling strings. You understand? Like a puppeteer.

Because in the shooting range and in the world, a lot of people can pull triggers. And in the puppet business, a lot of people can pull strings. But how many have the heart to do both?

Yeah, a lot of people say it, but how many actually do it? Is not the gun that gives you power is the heart, nephew.

Pusher

push, push, push, pushing– is the pusher man
pushing all the colors of the rainbow with his hand
he pushed the white, he pushed the green
and all the colors in between
even pushes purple and the tangerine
Mandarin and aspirin
he pushes yellow, red and brown
leafy matter from the ground
pushes tar that's gooey black
liquefied or still intact
then pushes back and pushes fro
pushes plants to push to grow
pushing rainbows from his hand,
keep it pushing pusher man

Like an Acupuncture Parlor

beware of evil men and women
who look not like the way they are inside
foul, foul, and no limit to their level of cowardness
for they are putrid within to the core or more
someday you might meet men like these
and they might giggle, remark and whisper of you
and of your approaches towards life
they will also smile for you as hostesses are forced to do
and like a greeter who detests his unglorified position
they will hate to smile at you
and will measure your victories by their failures
beware of evil men and women who look not
like the way they are inside

Archer

My last arrow for the pharaoh
shrapnel, through my flesh and apparel.
The final stand.
Cornered in this narrow corridor.
No reinforcements.
Dead, pale men, and dead horses
Is all that remains of my military forces.
My last stand
Outside the barren fortress
Among my brethren's corpses.
Eyes are blurry focused
on that which they idolize,
I'm trying to finalize my opus.
In the cold mist,
I saved my last arrow for the pharaoh.

No Appointment

Pale, fractured people.

Sexy peasant women flock.

Malnutritioned children, some in strollers, some on foot,

pushed by single mothers.

Grandmas, under dressed, sit on teal chairs.

Rows of broken folks— wait to hear their name called.

A man in jogging shorts and t-shirt is standing in line for window: A.

"Do you have appointment? Asks the Asian little lady.

"Who's your social worker?"

"Jesus Christ." I sighed. Damn, I got a pretty, goth, Asian social worker.

Light conversation and the occasional sinful eye between us

is all we share.

She helps me with my issues, and I thankfully depart.

In between now and thirty days, I shall have some food stamps.

Poem-lessness

Why am I a poet?
Because that's what I am
It is all I've known to be
I am not a poet
It's just poetry is me
Feeling superb
I am the answer to poem-lessness
Poetry is me.
She wears me like a costume
And leaves me like a classroom
She's led me into friendships
And held me when I'm helpless
She comes to me in seasons
Like a bonus for the janitor
And whispers sweet somethings
In an iambic pentameter
The Excalibur type caliber
I'm an infinite parameter
A puppet for Her Majesty
A foot or meter
A unit of poetry is like jump rope
Each jump is a foot
if you start at the jump, it is stressed
If it ends on the jump, it's unstressed
No apology for my analogy
While artistic hands have shaped my works
Into cups of couplets stanzas verbs...
But in essence, I am words
I am the feeling of these words
I am formless like I am rule-less,

Though some shape me into sonnets
I'm the soul inside these phonics
Like a phoenix illuminating
Dark abandoned faces
I'm the substance in the phrases
Poetry is talking through me
I'm the mother of dictation
Giving birth to inspiration
I am blood in circulation
In the rivers of your body
I am art inside of heart
But I'm the heart, inside of art
Neither ignorant nor smart
What I am is not important
I am everyone and no one
I'm a newly written poem
I have traveled to your soul
I am yours for you to hold
I am yours for you to mold
For your hands to take control
I, am, poetry

Pee Poe

People who pass me
Some, they are stranger than I am
At times
Look at those cowardly faces
What if our souls could be racist?
What then?
Meeting these strangers
As strange as their questions
What can be stranger than
Strangers or strange-ettes
Strange as my poetry methods
In wars that apply different weapons...
It's strange
How the eternal can change
In just seconds
It is so, so, so... so strange

Pee Poe 2

Still looking at people that pass me
some they are stranger than me
faceless expressions that last me
show me what's worthy to see
looking at people familiar
glance at the people that's strange
everyone strange in this new place
each one as unique as me
we all seem comfortable enough
to inhabit our surroundings
with a levelheaded coolness
only falling stars possess
but how easily we fall
for an all-in-one shot
if fucking up was an art, I'd be DaVinci
in fact, if fucking up was a craft
I'd be Sylvia Plath
I'm still looking at people who pass me
some they are stranger than I am at times
look at those cowardly faces
what if our souls could be racist
what then?
It's strange how the eternal can change
in just seconds
it is so, so, so strange

Painted Faces

painting faces
with hopes that I may change
their faceless impressions,
vague less expressions, tasteless suggestions
but how ego would I be
without painting based on me
painting faces
hoping to reflect the prevailing races
to illustrate the phases
we deny ourselves through gazes
painting faces
to preserve the moods of certain ages
these peculiar, pasty agents
beautified as painted faces

Muscle Shoals

Muscle Shoals souls with stones
my, my Mexican bones
time, old time, keeps changing
you never know when you're making history
Keith Richards tunes with rooms
hit recording capital of the world
Rick Hall shitting on high cotton
wild horses flying free as birds
the river water flows in Muscle Shoals
I got that bassy kick drum muddy blue sound
from the songs sung from the lady in the river
the words and notes trinkle
sprinkle and ripple and triple
inside the top layers of water of my soul
speak to me Skynyrd
the sound, my sound, I found
down South and the sound found me
in the waters of rivers that connects
from Muscle Shoals wild horse
joined through a musical universal accord
it's the same soul we share which takes us there
let the music play

Le' Formula

Ladies,
will you please leave your men at home?
I'll tell you how I made my style my own.
Men,
refrain from bringing wives.
It will only complicate your lives.
Youngsters,
bring your homies, please.
I'll tell you how I got my steez.
Promise not to tell a soul.
And I'll tell you all I know.
Never copy no one else.
It takes skills to be yourselves.
Dedication is the key.
That will set your talent free.
Patience is a mastered trait.
All things great, take time to make.
Do all of these things, and you too will know.
How it feels to steal the show.

Three Dots

At age 17, my brother drove a midnight blue Chevy Nova and was an active gang member and a tattoo artist. I was like 5 years old at the time. I would go into the garage and quietly observe and listen to my brother and his friends who would hang among the dusty cardboard boxes that read words like Christmas lights and Lulu's stuff, written on them with black marker. They would listen to Mary Wells, Credence, War, Zap & Roger, and sing along to them. Sometimes, they would smoke, other times they would drink, sometimes they had girls over, other times, they would do all three. Regardless of all the drinking, smoking and other activities that went on in the garage, ultimately, this was my brother's sacred ground because this is where he tattooed.

Even though my brother and his friends were still teenagers they were some scary looking dudes who wore creased baggie pants, white tee shirts, hair nets, and dark sunglasses. They had scars, tattoos, and bandanas hanging out from their back pockets.

My brother did not want me hanging around the garage, especially when he was tattooing his friends. He'd kick me out, but I'd sneak back in. I was around my brother and his friends so often that I knew most of their names. Gang members have the craziest names. Seemed like they were either named after animals, villains, cartoon characters, personality traits, and physical appearance. For example, there was Scrappy, Woody, Daffy, Smokey, Yogi, Scooby, Shaggy, Gumby, Casper, Popeye, Creeper, Sneaky, Silent, Green Eyes, Evil, Wicked, Danger, Trouble, Chico, Chuco, Chucky, Chino, Shorty, Tiny, Lil Man, Peewee, Dopey, Happy, Grumpy, Smiley, Chimp, Night Owl, Spider and Stomper, just to name a few.

I enjoyed watching my brother architect his blueprint sketches and trace them onto flesh before he began the actual tattoo. I was so persistent on being in the garage with my brother and his friends, that one day my brother told me that if I ever came in the garage again while he is tattooing his friends that he would poke me with his tattoo machine. Then, he would turn on the machine and place it near my ear to scare me. The machine sounded like a mechanical mosquito buzzing about and disturbing my childish tranquility. Despite my brother's efforts to scare me away, I still wouldn't leave the garage. Instead, I would stare at my brother as he injected stab after stab after stab of China Ink onto his friends bleeding, bronze flesh. On one particular occasion there were only my brother and two of his friends, Smiley and Chuco; on this day my brother was tattooing Chuco's back and teaching Smiley how to make a tattoo machine.

The tattoo machine was obviously homemade and consisted of:
- a small motor (those days it was from a Walkman)
- one square Duracell battery
- a clear, papermate pen cut in half
- a sewing needle, or guitar string
- black electric tape

As he proceeded to carve away flesh, Chuco, squinting, took small swallows from a clear bottle of tequila and my brother seemed uncomfortable at the fact that I was in the garage. The first and second time that he asked me to leave, I walked out of the garage momentarily and then came back in. By the third time he told me to leave I just ignored him. I remember my brother stopping the tattoo machine, looking towards me and signaling with his hand for me to come over here. I walked over and he grabbed the spare needle from his little brown duffel bag and opened a new bottle of dark blue China Ink. He dipped the needle halfway into the bottom of the ink bottle and grabbed my right hand and with the ink-soaked needle he punctured 3 rapid and consecutive wounds, into my infantile skin, like a tiny pyramid, on my right hand at the point where the index and thumb touch if you were making an L like Loser. "Now you can hang around," said my brother, as I ran crying out of the garage, knocking down empty beer bottles filled with gum wrappers and cigarette butts. I dashed into the house and tried to wash off the odd mixture of dark blue ink and bright red blood into a white porcelain sink.

My mother and father were at work and my sisters were in school. This meant that 5-year-old me had my brother, the tattooing gang member, for a babysitter. By the time my mother came home from work I had forgotten about the tattoo and did not mention it to her. It was the next morning, while eating cereal, when she noticed the three small dots tattooed on my right hand. My mother gasped for breath as she stared at my little tattooed hand, covering her mouth with both palms. After invoking several Saints, the Virgin Mary, Joseph, Jesus, and baby Jesus, the next name out of her mouth was my brother's name, "MIGUEL!!!"

My sisters, who had also just learned about the tattoo, began gossiping among themselves and picking up my hand and passed it around like a hot potato. I heard my mother shouting at my brother in the garage. Not the usual shouting; this was a strange form of shouting which was followed by silence. My sisters quietly listened to my mother's words. After another one-minute round of shouting there was a loud sound from a car door slamming shut followed by an igniting car engine and tires burning rubber as they sped off. My sisters quietly proceeded to eat breakfast as my mother walked back into the kitchen with tears in her eyes. That day, the Cuban lady from next door babysat me, and I would not see my brother again 'til I was 13 years old.

A few weeks later I started kindergarten. It was my first day of school and I was the only 5-year-old with a tattoo.

CHAPTER 5

HARDHEARTED

Onion Head

Scrunchy tied bun
Honey bun wrapper
Cinnamon lips
Roll of twenties in her bra
Blunt roaches on soda cup ashtrays
Bike horn grocery cart
Smells of mangos on sticks powdered in chili red dust
Corn on sticks with mayo and Parmesan
Hard to choose when it is her asking you
Nothing on the news matters to you except the winning number on the
mega millions
Hotdog gourmet dinners
Dripped mustard on Sunday shoes
You only went to church on Ash Wednesdays
You thought the tooth fairy left you a fake twenty under your
suspicious pillow
Look how you have grown
Inside-out sweats and unmatching slippers
Hair in a bun, like an onion
That is how I see you...
In my heart.

Of My Dreams

She is the woman of my dreams
Though beautiful women surround me
Infinitely, her beauty is beyond comparison
Though she loses her feelings for me at times
I will never leave her heart
I refuse to
Though she breaks from aches my words have made on her
I mend her with actions that speak louder
And clearer than any love poems ever whispered
WWith minted breath upon her ear and neck
She, the woman of my dreams
And I, her dreamer
Though beautiful goddesses and queens
And princesses, at times, have stumbled
In my presence with inviting eyes
Of celestial divinity
They could never reach her essence
She is the woman of my dreams come true
A déjà vu times déjà vu
Of ultraviolet, baby-blue
And infrared, and dark maroon
Of all things grand and all things new
And even though beautiful women
Shall forever tread the grounds
Of my undeserving world
To me, none but she, shall ever be
The woman of my dreams

I am in Love with a Goddess

She is slim and she's a genius
as beautiful as God
With legs like golden trees
that stretch from earth up to the heavens
and breasts plump as the fruits on tropical trees
I tongue kiss her from neck to feet
Her eyes shiny as black diamonds
they seek me out and I feel touched every time she looks upon me
Like the sun touched me
I am in love with a goddess
who is not modest and
finds it hard to be honest
My queen is a genius
beautifully hideous
of honey bronze brilliance
my Highness vagina's
the goddess of *hainas*

the flyest of pilots
the livest of violets
the Princess of jazmins
the Empress of kiss prints
tonguing her clitoris
kissing her squinched lips
lunar eclipses
messy and sexy
breastfeed me bless me
strawberry Nestle
the princess of passion
of *paisas* in fashion

a kiss on her lashes
my queen is an engineer
hold her firmly by the air
kiss her gently by the ear
licking you through your panties
then pull them to the side
then kiss it slowly like I'm eating an ice cream cone
that begins melting as I tongue it with eyes closed
and soft moans of deep low tones deep slow
I'm going to come inside your soul

Beautifully

What is missing from my night?
Something beautiful to write.
What is missing from my day?
Something beautiful to say.
Beauty be so far and distant.
Almost seeming non-existent.
Dressed in silk.
Black As Guilt.
Or colored milk.
She is beautiful regardless.
And her room adorned of starlets.
The desire of all artists.
Patron Saint of timid harlots is she.
The mother goddess of all talents.
The remainder of all balance.
She is beauty.
She is beautiful.
She is fire. Only colder
In the heart of her beholder.
She is Passion's rightful owner.
Beauty. Unexcited yet delighted.
Arrives late and uninvited.
Her regalia ultraviolet.
Baby blue and infrared.
She is ice but only hotter.
Just above the boil of water.
She is everything and nothing.
She is kindness in a war.
In the nuclear debris
Of a certain war to be,

When all trees and flowers fall
She's the White Rose rising tall.
Through the fiery sting of snow.
Where there's nothing, she is all.
She is beautiful to see.
Beauty she will always be.
Celebrated beautifully.

Bird

chirpy birds that chirp in trees
let me share you my disease
I can hear you in the background
flapping wings upon the leaves
writers block my book release
ideal prince and crook of thieves
hated by these heartless harlots
queen of garments shoplift sprees
dreams of garbage arrow postage
streets of carnage never closest
hit me girl and give me dosage
fill my batteries with voltage
praise your temple like the Toltecs
at your service like I'm your bitch
but I'm not
I'm more like birds
but instead of chirps it's words

let me show you my disease
chirpy birds that chirp in trees
I can hear you in the background
flapping wings upon the leaves
mundane detailed book release
like an inmate to the streets
once confined in flesh and mind
now his crime sprees have increased
deprived of time by frozen minutes
a demigod of ghosts and spirits
coughing 'til my throat is clearest
blood, ink, quills, rhymes, poison lyrics

art reveals thy chosen limits
gaudy fields of voiceless critics'
noiseless crickets
more like birds
but instead of chirps it's words.
it's for the birds

Waking Up from Dreams of Her

woke up from dreams of her, blurs of her
now I'm awake
sleepwalking dreams of her... calling her name
oh lady, won't you... come for me
and keep for me... company
and make sweet, dark secrets hush worthy
skin visions, she's on her way to my way
I woke up from dreams of her, blurs of her
now I'm awake
peach rose petals, silk; your kisses of milk
is this love or is this guilt,
or is it time for tides to wash away
the sandcastles we built
woke up from dreams of her
in which she was a marionette
and I would cut the strings from her
and we would walk through time, all the time
to reach each of her
but I woke up from dreams of her
rubbed my eyes from blurs of her
and now I am awake from her
in bed, saying to myself
she was just a dream

Men

to the men who call themselves men
whose gluttonous fingers forcefully mishandled flowers
who do not wish to be plucked by you
for you are far too brutish
and would only cause her damage
but never have you tried to nurture her
and feed her water
nor did you tend to her
nor placed her near proper sunlight
nor trimmed her leaves
nor removed the weeds from her surroundings
nor did you ever attempt to strengthen
the life she held inside
instead you made her petals fall
and caused her to subside
men who call themselves men
can't handle being rejected by a beautiful young rose
her petals are not meant for your touch
they close
you are not the man meant to pick her from her garden
but you are the one who caused her petals to be hardened
men who call themselves men
who see a flower planted standing tall
with firm stem and solid roots
and want to pick her out the soil where she resides in
you are intrigued by the beauty of her nature
and can't control your primal urges
to devour, to consume, to abuse
when your main concern should be to preserve
instead you try to take then break

that which you did not deserve

trying to force that which is only earned

men who call themselves men

and give real men a bad name

no green thumb just green

you are more locust than pesticide

let her grow for you could never appreciate her petals puckered

your hoofs would only trample her towards doom

for you she will not bloom

sunflower seeds upon the moon

a flower?

if only cowards mustered up powers to startle her

a ranch hand could never be a gardener

if you had her planted in your yard

she would wither in your winter

every time you try to pluck her from the ground

another splinter

she is not for you

now let her grow

men who call themselves men

who curse at flowers with mouths like sinkholes

if you cannot appreciate her essence

her naturalistic monumental presence

let her be in nature

as she's meant to... free

men who take what is not given

who can't appreciate beauty in its natural environment

have the flowers in these gardens all denied you?

and have them all regret the day if they ever tried you

now I've tied you to a bouquet

of all the flowers that you shamed
afraid to ask for help or even to complain
for fear of your deceitful ways
that may defame their name
these flowers are not ours
we must shelter them from showers
we must treasure them and guard them
from the plagues that aim to harm them
men who call themselves men
but only to pretend
this is your magnum opus
I came to bring you roses

Valentine's Ghost

ghosts of her they haunt me so
once she used to rock me slow
now she's simply just a phase
in the error of my ways
used to be my ghetto queen
fancy product of a dream
now she's just a scareless ghost
blurry vision of the coast
I still squint in disbelief
rising up from out the deep
pulling arrows from her spine
it's the ghost of Valentine

Moe Moe

summer spells in cheap motels
where bibles look like pamphlets
deadly curves I crashed in hers
and covered them with blankets
what a night the summer type
with sweat at 3:00 AM
how the hell in cheap motel
we ended up again

Waiting for Butterflies

She became another ex. Along with the others.
On my wall of discarded things.
Once highly guarded now disregarded things.
From within this measured darkness.
I allow sunlight to touch my neck.
Soft and warm stings like being kissed by desert lizard's lips.
She paroled my prison. Right before the midnight hour of execution.
She's found freedom now. In her so desired world of infant men and
elder dogs.
She.
Found what lies beyond me.
Agreed to a lifetime contract. Bound by blood.
To poison daffodils. And putrid orchids.
And I am a purified deity
fatherless....
Bastarded by her love.
Sitting....
Next to caterpillars....
Waiting....
For the butterflies to form.

Nothing from You

I don't want nothing from you anymore
I'm tired of waiting for you to trust me.
Where does one my age meet freaks nowadays?
I rather have that than you...
The unrequested feeling of truth caresses me like soft hands touching
my face from behind
And I sigh... for truth favors me tonight.
Regardless of how mustard and horseradish fetish relish her taste to
my tongue may be.
I rather have her
For she need not lie to satisfy.
I want nothing from you.
Nothing. Not a look or an insinuation of thought, I don't want to know
you anymore,
like a spontaneous amnesia from an icy brain freeze in the cherry
middle of a seven eleven.
I'm cool,
I don't want nothing from you.

She is Super Ma'am

Super Ma'am, Super babe,
Super woman, Super Dame
Super chick, Super *haina*
the return of the vagina
she is Super Ma'am,
bringing sister hood back
to her sisters held back
escape from your Mac, Maybelline,
Revlon, mascara eyelash prison camp
disregard the over-sexual
focus on the intellectual
piece of meat she leaves behind
a piece of ass but Peace of Mind
when will all the bastards cease
and recognize a masterpiece
Super girl, Super sheera,
Super woman, Super diva
Super ma'am, Super Mama
the pre, the post, and pro-Madonna
the martyr of a lonely post
the mother, daughter, Holy Ghost
Amen.
A(wo)men.
prone to suffer
but did not cook the final supper
Miss Messiah, Jesus-ina;
or the passion of Christina
supersede these super bitches,
super dumb and superstitious
super major, nomenclature

Mother Earth and Mother Nature
Melt the glaziers, flood the ocean
fill the oxygen with poison
let the fixers mend their fixtures,
and the Misters shed their whiskers
messing with my Super Sisters

Ode Owed to the Poetess

With humility and honor I proudly touch the heavens
who permit me to speak of subjects and entities so divine,
the angels and devils must both pay attention.
May the most high appoint muses to guide my pen and keystroke
as I embark on this journey to pay homage to the promise,
the premise, of a promised land accomplished,
the poetess, queen of scripters. My divine dear strength,
scripter and inscriber of thoughts and sentiments
far too poised for men and boys.
I bow to your feet, queen of keyboards, pens and speech.
Princess of proverbs, Duchess of dialect.
Her pronouns are pronouns, unable to precede or assign description
to this vicious vision of non-fictitious visage
of unscripted digits, a crimson vixen of prescriptions written,
lotus of poetics which the orchid orbits,
the enormous smorgasbord of poems' corpses.
Queen bee rebuttals that make puddles oceans.
No nuisance nor nonsense or loose ends synopsis.
Princess of progress that pricks in the process
the promise of bomb threats, the calmness of convicts,
the conflicts on convents, accomplished as conquests is she.
The Countess of quantum countenance,
the remnants of fragranced roses,
the Empress of golden temperance,
the goddess of prolific artists.
Since you are naturally modest allow me to be honest on your behalf.
Let me give you your roses before they wilt into dry petals,
let me kiss your creative fingertips mother of composition,
sister of contradiction.
You are the inspiration when I'm down and out.

This I compose to a rose.
The prophetic Princess of prose
amongst high priests and shamans,
brujos glucose,
eres la Reyna curandera.
Medicine woman
supreme nurse of free verse,
let us join chromosomes and produce rebirths.
Drop TNT by the megatons,
Long live the Queens of the Renaissance.

As I Loved Her

To the woman who said
she never met a man
with so much sentiment I say
I'm sorry that you never met someone
who loves you just because of you.
Someone who would leave his world for yours,
or takes you out of yours to bring you into his, in an instant.
Someone who ignores when the waitress smiles a bit too long,
or her conversation is a bit too extensive.

You never had one
who sets those women straight,
and puts them in their place in your presence.

I'm sorry you've never been
woken up to your clit licked
eyes opened, face to face, tongue kiss twist
with interlocked fingers gripped
stare into your eyes eclipse
I almost forgot about the kids type bliss.

To the woman who does not understand
how I can love, get my heart broken,
and still love again, all I can say is this:

I'm sorry that no one made you their goddess
and worshipped you from feet to head.
Poems read in bed
and composed chapbooks with your name,
and wrote sonnets about your cooking,
or kissed every single inch of your back.

I'm sorry you've never been loved like that,
that you could never comprehend a man
with sentiments such as I,
who is not ashamed nor have to lie
of how I loved with such emotions, deep as oceans,
like one loves seeing pictures of mom and dad
when they were cool. When they were still happy
and family photo albums made sense.

I'm sorry that no one has ever touched you from across the room
only by looking at you, without saying any words.
I'm sorry no one ever told you that in this whole universe
there exists no flower that could be synonymous with you.
I'm sorry no one ever made you feel like
the most beautiful woman in the room, in a room full of beautiful women.
To that woman or man who doesn't understand,
how a man can love so deeply without fear or envy,
without perversions or lustful priorities, I say this:

I'm sorry you haven't got to love the way I loved,
maybe if you did you would understand why I feel as I feel.
But since you never loved no one the way I've loved,
I can't hold it against you
not being able to comprehend a love such as mine.
I can't hold it against you
that you don't understand the emotional extremities of my being,
for you never reached such boundless duties of humanity.
The ability to freely, fully appreciate another.
I'm sorry no one ever gave you all with just one word,
and bombarded you with compliments on your worst days,
and dug you up from graves which you have dug yourself in,
or lifted you from the darkest pits of ruin,
when the world had discarded you in landfills of forgotten rubbish.

Lifted you with calloused hands and rough fingertips
and told you that you are everything,
you are worth the struggle, the pain and all adversity.
I'm sorry no one ever loved you,
as I loved her.

Mixtapes & Mistakes

Her name was Veronica Daily but her stage name was Dime Piece, a tall, half-Mexican half-Italian former fashion model turned rapper with eyes like opals, lips like rose petals and hair as long and black as the night sky.

"This is Breeze," said my friend and beat-maker named Pyro, as he introduced us for the first time.

Immediately, there was a spark between us. An instant connection. A mutual respect for each other's craft. Small talk between us and one of Pyro's beats and one hour later we had a complete song. Till this day it's one of my all-time favorite songs and one of my most popular songs as well as hers.

Everyone in the studio was excited. It was on everyone's tongue but Pyro let it out first, saying, "Aah Shit! DIME PIECE and BREEZE!!!!"

I looked at her and she smiled in agreement. We stepped outside to get some air and Veronica and I began to compliment each other on the dope track we had just wrote and recorded together. She had a shine in her black pearl eyes that hypnotized and forced vision to commit itself to her. What can I say to you without smiling? Nothing.

A smile is present as long as she is present in my presence
in my present she is presents gifts of precious incandescence
light in essence life possesses in the mind there lies intentions
in the heart there lies receptions misconstrued then misdirection's
she is reaching for her weapon, I am reaching for my weapon
we are either made in heaven or well matched for Armageddon

Damn, for one second there I was lost. Absorbed into the obscurity of her eyes that also shine; like oiled lagoons.

She said she paints in her spare time. Let me paint your spare time, I suggested.

She agrees, we connect, exchange numbers like recipes.

Inside Pyro's dimly lit studio we sit. Sharing beers and mixed drinks.

Silence is appreciated more when she's around.

Her and her friend now must go. It was so nice to meet you though.

As their vehicle departs, my friend Pyro looks at me and says, "Don't do it. Keep it strictly friendship, don't fuck up the chemistry."

But I did not listen to Pyro.

I called her the following night. She invited me to her place where we talked and listened to beats and ideas for songs and we had so much chemistry that we decided that we would do an album together.

We agreed. When Veronica tried to get a little close to me I had to shut her down and remind her that we have an album to put together and could not let personal feelings get in the way of artistry. She agreed, for now, but I could tell she was really starting to like me. And her best friend liked me. She thought I was a good guy.

So Veronica and Me begin to get a bit closer and closer. She invited me out with her homegirls for her birthday.

"Yea we are going to perform in Pasadena, opening up for Inspectah Deck from the Wu Tang. And after the show we can all hang out," she said.

I hesitated at first, not wanting to add fuel to a fire that burned between us, but then decided that I would join them.

We all rolled in the same car. I have to admit, it was fun being the only guy riding in a car full of female rap chicks.

They played their set, killed it, and then we jetted off to get some tacos and some more drinks. I was riding with Dime Piece's friends and fellow artists. It was Gavalyn, Colombian Gold, Ms. Lee, and Top Dime. All very talented, very cool and very beautiful women. They were the coolest group of women you could ever meet. I felt like they accepted me in their group and I felt Veronica, little by little, wanting to get closer and closer to me.

What is she thinking? I thought to myself. She knows we can't fuck around. We are working on an album.

One night, Veronica invited me over to listen to some beats that we might choose from for our album. I must admit, that going over to her house made me nervous because she was such a good-looking woman so it would be hard being around her for a few hours and trying not to fall for her.

I was playing a dangerous game. Maybe tonight I will tell her that I will be taking a break from this project because I am starting to tell that she is falling for me, I thought to myself. Actually, I had started falling for her too.

That was it. I had to call it off.

I arrived at Veronica's and said something like "Hey I can't really stay today, just wanted to tell you something."

She said, "Before you say anything, can you help me out with something?"

"With what?" I said.

She led me to her room and showed me her closet. "I'm trying to transform my closet into a vocal recording booth."

I looked her in her eyes and before she finished speaking she smiled, then said, "Just kiss me already."

We started kissing and static electricity transmitted between us. Her lips: an electric pulp of flower petals, wet. The forbidden fruit devoured upon her bed. Her long silky legs like the arms of a great octopus, wrapped around my torso as we wrestled for control of each other like two gangs fighting over territory. Her beautiful eyes shined like black pearls at the bottom of some dark unexplored ocean. Her breasts perfect fruits hanging from the branches of the most forbidden tree in the garden of Eden. Lush and perky they stood, the way angels' might. Night progressed and we cared not. Time might as well have stopped and the sun and moon paused. All things outside our intimate parameter had ceased to exist.

Tomorrow I will tell her what I came to tell her, I told myself. Tomorrow I will tell her that this cannot go on. Tomorrow I will tell her that I am starting to fall for her like she is falling for me. And that cannot happen.

Tomorrow I will tell her that my heart already belongs to someone else.

CHAPTER 6

VILLAIN

An Honest Woman

I, am an Honest Woman, so you will believe me when I say,
I have been on the top of this so-called "man's world."
I've walked bare feet on wet, glass ceilings, breastfeeding, pregnant,
with a baby on one arm and a book in the other,
hair in a bun held with scrunchy.
My hair is both curly and straight.
My skin: a wall of silk of different tones like church bells or seasons.
I am an African, Asian, Arian, Latina, Indigenous woman.
I've been denied the right to own property, the right to vote,
the right to study, the right to hope, the right to dream,
the right to lead, the right to write, but never more.
What if one day, someday, on God's green earth,
I decide to deny the right to give birth,
what then? If births should end.
I control the fate of men.
I am womanhood's reprise. The universe between my thighs.
Joyous hymns are in my cries. Futures gleam within my eyes.
I am woman, gun in hand, mother of the son of man.
Mother nature's pretty danger, cultivator of God's land.
I am the spiritual, sexual, intellectual being.
It is I, the pyramid's eye, that's all seeing.
I am man's wife and God's baby daughter.
I'm the tree of life, humanities godmother.
I'm heavens most precious Angel that can switch
into the most evil, devilish bitch.
I am the temptress, mistress, gangstress, Princess,
queen, and Empress, restless pimpstress.
I have been, I am, history's unsung hero.
Blamed for all of human evil.
They say I'm the first to sin.
They say I was birthed by him.

From his rib I was conceived;
he the day and I the Eve,
I the weak and He the strong.
He the right and I the wrong. He the pollen, I the seed.
He shall lead and I shall bleed. He shall fertilize the earth;
I shall bear the pain of birth. For I am woman, conned, betrayed.
Cheated-on and made to blame.
I've been worshiped more than the usual suspect:
flowers of fresh orchids.
They have made me out to be lethal as the silent Sea.
Silent me. An autumn blossom. winter solstice, splintered Lotus.
Wonder if they even noticed when I wrote this from the bottom.
My ideas are feared severe, I had to buy a man to jot them
or to merely talk about them, the cold touch of mausoleums.
Because I am an honest woman, from within the very omen
from the entrails of my Ovum. Master of a handsome moment,
beauty of a language stolen, masquerade in jade importance,
for the sake of earthly orbits and early births. A future dormant.
I am, an honest woman.

"Of"

The world is not for me.
Though I often allow it passage into the wilderness of my heart.
Vague and cockeyed it flashes its trophies and ill-accumulated
victories as if I gave a fuck.
Tyranny is returned here.
In well decorated gift wrap paper it arrives.
The long-awaited package.
Sign and initial here and it's yours.
But the world is not for me.
It is the "on-sale" gift exchange that you must re wrap and re gift
All its marquee citizens are monstrous.
Lucid dreamers of fantastic giveaways.
Get rich products of adversity.
The ravished embryo undeveloped.
The near rotted cantaloupe with gnats abundant.
Repugnant leftovers that lacked in nutrients.
But the world is not for me.
I'm from a simpler time
Where getting a whipping was not
considered child abuse but tough love.
Pain made sense. Where Saturday morning cartoons existed.
And the triumph of our shared love was well established.
Nowadays, my well-being is at the mercy of my captors.
Those who pose as allies yet fed us poison in the form of entrées.
Audacious bastards, they sell us overpriced cake and help us eat it too.
I attempt to feel at home, but it does not feel as such.
A strange dictator reigns in place of my rationale.
We are all out of heroes
And our elders have left us the key
To this old and tattered marketplace.
Everything your eye can see,
Of the world, is not for me.

Rotten Apples

People of today, let your children play.
Free them from the prison
Of their plasma screen display.
iPod children, iPad teens,
iTunes Adams, iPhone Eves.
Adam bit the apple that contains no seeds,
Megabyte the fruits that produce no trees.
The females and e-males, with sad, blue faces.
In turn, couldn't learn, from their MacBook pages.
The roots of creation in the Garden of Eden,
Are ethernet cables, in the Garden of Steven.
The iMachiavellian can write you a war map,
A knack, to adapt with a universal format.
Running out of seeds, and land to grow a tree on.
The icon for a peon is painted faded neon.
iPod babies, with USB umbilical.
Connected to the mother board's womb,
through electrical components.
Prenatal, quarter-inch cable through the navel,
lullabies downloaded to unsupervised cradles.
We use smart phones to do stupid shit,
While capital profits corner the markets,
For innovations that provide us low progress.
People of today let your children play.
Technology in shackles.
Instead of food for thought,
They've fed us rotten apples.

Sheltered

Is there a shelter for battered men?
for their bruises are within
probably shattered up his toys
abusive men from battered boys
still, that gives him no excuse
for the physical abuse
probably battered as a child
kept it stashed behind the smile.
Sometimes they grow up to be
just like all they know and see.

Though my sister's open eyes
could not let her realize
the real price her kids must pay
for she felt she had to stay.
For the pain she held inside
the best makeup could not hide
what about the kids that see
what they never want to be
made to choose at 3:00 AM
"Go with mommy or with him."

When the mom and daddy fights
are the children's saddest nights.
Walls and pillows aren't thick enough
for children's ears to hide behind.
She knew she didn't have to stay
but she couldn't go away.
Mom and daddy do the crime
which the children now must pay
they pretend amongst the norm
with regrets of being born.

And they go about their day
like a normal child would play.
Play alone or with a friend
wishing day would never end,
for they know that in the night
that's when dad and mommy fight.
Battered men and battered boys
do not always shatter toys,
but their bruises are within
is there a shelter for battered men?

Sacred Grounds

Ladies and gentlemen,
at this particular moment in space and time
you are now standing on sacred ground.
At this moment the ground that your feet rests upon
is a vast vessel of virtues and verses.
You are in the presence, ladies and gentlemen,
of thoughts profound.
You are now in the palace of poetic prowess and potency.
Right now, resting on these walls,
you are surrounded
by some of the most beautiful words ever composed
and put together by the hand of a human being
accompanied by works of some of the legends of the past.
But you are also surrounded by some of the works
of the legends of the future.
And though you may not realize it, ladies and gentlemen,
you too are at this very moment taking part in history.
Behold, the works of the greats sit amongst you
and call this place their home.
The place that makes you ask yourself this question:
what to do after dreams come true?
The home to the humble and discreet
to the ambitious and flamboyant
academic scholars and streetwise educators,
where the academic and streetwise share the same vision,
where both rich and poor alike
breathe life into the same mic.
This place opens its doors to all who wish to enter.
This is a sacred place
where children have played

and have spilled buckets of laughter,
where young men and women have spoken poems that
have opened minds from the once closed gates of ignorance.
You are now standing in the gathering place
of thinkers and visionaries
who do not require eyes to have vision,
which could gaze beyond the present time
and into futures near and distant.
This is sacred ground on which authors are birthed.
This is sacred training ground from which among us
will arise legends of futures soon to be established.
This is The Sims Library of Poetry:
influence of literature that defies time, the ultimate time capsule that
contains the largest collection of poetry books in the West Coast.
And tonight we add one more to that collection.

Jellybeans

Junior high brown teens don't want to eat beans no more.
No gracias mama, no thanks mother.
I'm eating imitation cereal for breakfast this morning.
Bid me good day mother, like you usually do
and remind me how lucky I am to attend this ghetto ass, American
public inner-city school.
And how is school? Mother asks.
He replies, it's cool, it's cool.
But deep inside, his heart screams, "only if you knew"
his outside was Cleveland brown, his insides are dodger blue.
I found out my own race can be prejudice too.
In Mexico they called me Pocho, Chicano, Sellout Mexicano.
But here they call me wetback, border hopper, pancho's giveaway
thrift store shopper.
But it's one word that kills me most.
Is the source which holds the strength, is the one I must accept
and so proudly represent: the bean,
rich in protein, yes you can call me beaner,
I can eat them every day for my breakfast lunch and dinner.
Beaner, beans by the pound, or by the teener
no imitation crabmeat cracks on the femur.
I have beans of Jelly and beans of soy,
beans of Lima and beans of joy.
I'm a beanie baby; became a bean teen.
During droughts when I sprout,
I prefer Mr. Bean.
Beaner. Never mind my demeanor.
Fertilize mother earth,
drop my seed in between her
throwing pesticide on my hereditary genes,

under pressure trying to turn us into refried beans.
Looking for a slice of the bean pie
in a melting pot, getting deep fried
knee deep in bean dip, tortilla chip dream,
tried to dip crackers, they lose saltine.
I'm a beaner; don't be seduced by the street talk
born to kill giants like Jack and the Beanstalk.
Jack of all trades, Jack in the box,
blackjack 21; Jack on the rocks.
The bean rich in protein, no saltine.
Mom's warming up tortillas,
I'm bringing back the beans.

Amiri's Theory

Legacy of legend which I've never met
never heard or seen, yet, never will forget.
May I speak it clearly: Amiri Baraka theory.
Surprised?
How Mexican lips spit black thoughts
because brotherhood is beyond black power or brown pride.
All of Amiri's verses: universes. One verse.
We honor thee in women's month for Goddesses give birth
to men that travel earth and plant seeds beneath the dirt.
Ask to reverse a process and give rebirth to profits
and we are in the process of all that which is progress
no more I am the walrus, for now I am the man.
At times I've been the panther, the deer with broken antler.
A simple baggage handler; product of the past.
A product of adversity, Baraka university—
of gunpowder and potpourri, a spermicide and ovary.
For morons home runs hunting, but now I'm into bunting.
From master and the hunter I rather be the Butler
if choiced to be the coach, I'd rather be the Roach—
the teacher to approach. I never met Amiri.
But I know that what he gained and lost were both the same.
Giving up awards and all, in all our names.
What under Compton weather one man has brought together
can never be abolished can never be in vain
my tribute is indebted to all who earned the credit
for chaos and destruction is made for those who let it
and I have put my foot down and never put the book down
for ties that fail to bind us one day we all are hood bound.
My mother was a farm worker who earned a meager pay;
Let's show appreciation to women everyday.

We equally contribute an underrated tribute,
a legacy continued of struggle, love and sweat.
And though I never met him, I profit from his legend,
and though I never knew him I never will forget.
For those who may not hear me,
let me just speak clearly,
"live, love, and respect",
this is Amiri's theory.

Sky is Falling

Sky is falling on my planet
falling in and out of talent
falling stars falling leaves
falling in and out of peace
sky is crumbling coming down
scattered pieces all around
searching for a higher calling
feeling like the sky is falling

Lucifer's Logic

Many moods but none specific,
when I overstayed my visit
they decided my decisions
I decided not to kick it.
Now my boy Saint Michael is trippin'.
Called me blasphemous and wicked,
a demonic evil spirit.
He forgets my definition:
I'm the light that God permitted,
I'm the rays the sun emitted,
I'm the star beyond description,
I'm the seed from apples bitten,
from a tree that was forbidden,
I'm the one that God hath smitten,
I'm the crime that's not forgiven,
I'm the 'fuck you' of Thanksgiving.
I, the father of death's children,
from no paradise restricted.
I exist beyond the limit.
I'm the Prince of Darkness written, painted, spoken or envisioned.
I am religion's biggest Christian,
I am the sickness of your illness,
I am the cure to false prescriptions,
none but father, son, and spirit
are above my height or near it.
I am the Angel angel's mimic,
he whom God did not prohibit.
Life is given, I shall live it.
Endless in this deathless prison.

Some will fall and some have risen,
some have plucked without permission.
Some believe a snake that's hissin',
but to words they never listen.
Oh so easily submissive.
Who's to blame for your decision?
Eager to command distinction,
but are hardly worth extinction.
Can't see past your own reflection,
it is you, not I, who is wicked.
All I did was show you sinnin',
you're the one that's living in it.
You're the one that runneth with it,
You're the one who went and did it.
Now ashamed you won't admit it,
blaming me for your pandemic.
Everyone's a fucking critic,
you however, hypocritic.
I don't know why he's permitted
to live life the way you live it.
Many moods but none specific,
seems I've overstayed my visit.

Too Much of Anything

Started as a sweat that sprung from darkness
Creeping through me calmly in the stillness
Every bite goes deeper in my carcass
Filling up the hunger of my illness
Penetrating into my emotions
Salivating over my intentions
Growling at the sight of my devotions
Adding to the germs of my infection
Hanging from the edge of my salvation,
Clawing on the walls of my tradition,
Struggling away from my damnation,
Falling in the pits of my addiction.

You're Welcome

Tonight, me and the night are mutual
for we are both darker than usual.
Dark as fruit whose flesh is rotten
for a loss that's unforgotten.
Dark as guilt of fornication,
I am shame in checkered print.
Bulimia on Thanksgiving Day.
I'm the gangster in your church.
The Black Friday thief of 24-year-old girlfriends
who stand alone with styrofoam in hand.
Three cream and sugar kilos,
I am exaggeration at its worst,
addict doctors operating.
I am dark as hookers' rooms. I am infrared décor.
I am you when you are down, and I am I, when I am you.
I am voodoo dolls in Disneyland
or rapping drunk in Dixieland.
I'm the asshole king in Hyena Ville.
Revenger who refused to kill.
A spilled, white glop of vagisil on freshly ironed slacks.
I'm addictions correspondence,
I'm the scholar talking nonsense.
I'm a pervert with ideas,
the pollution from a Prius.
I'm a broken-hearted boyfriend
writing poems,
I am darkness.

The Writer's Block Theory

my down time offline no poetry writing season
beginnings are beginning and endings are revealing
somewhat too appealing or none too convincing
the cleansing of all corroded earthly feelings
for no longer kneeling is a new feeling
as all roads of religions lead to Jerusalem
so do the lines on this paper lead to one single source
the fact that writers block is a mental thing
it's only as real as you make it to be
there is no writer's block

Lefty Was Right

My memory is not the wondrous and abundant accredited source it once was but I think it was Uncle Carmelo, my dad's youngest brother, who used to say, "failure is the best teacher," and I've had my share of lessons taught throughout the various institutions of life. Uncle Carmelo's nickname was Lefty. As a teen, I can recall the time I saw him signing a get-well letter for grandma with his right hand and so I asked my father, "Hey dad, if Uncle Carmelo is right-handed why does everyone call him Lefty?"

My father smiled and told me, "Because he's never right."

I smiled back like an uncool kid trying to be cool would when trying to fit in a circle of cool kids. But nonetheless, Uncle Lefty was right this time; failure is the best teacher. And even though I haven't spoken to him for over a year and a half now, I still remember the last story he told me.

...

Alright keep it down, keep it down homes! So check it out fellas, we're going to go down the line starting with homeboy right here and I want you to tell me your name or what they call you, and where you are from. I'll start though; so yeah I'm the Rep in charge of the tier right here and they call me Lefty from Lynwood. Go ahead Homes, what they call you and where you from. (Fast forward 13 minutes.) Alright cool, so as you know we got to follow the "big homie rules" up in here. As long as you do your time, mind your own and don't step on nobody's toes you're going to be *Firme* and we ain't going to have no issues. If you do happen to slip up you get a one-time pass and a warning, but after that, I'm personally going to put hands on you and that's Mwah! (kisses his right-hand fingers in the form of a cross.) *Palabra*! Other than that just pay your dues, follow the rules, and you won't catch the county Blues.

Questions? No!? OK then, check it out, these two shitters on the end here are ours and the two pissers right next to it; that's the only ones you use. Also, don't ever come in the shower room bare foot, please don't do it. If you need shower shoes ask one of the homies to let you borrow some but don't ever leave your bunk bed barefoot, ever. The showers are for everyone to use but our shower times are from 5:00 to 7:00 AM in the mornings and from 6:00 to 8:00 PM at night, that's it. If you need to shave, brush your teeth, or whatever, only use these two sinks and that's it. Any questions on the shower room?... OK good. Follow me this way.

So if you need to use the phone you can use it anytime, but you must keep it down. The phone on the right and that one in the middle are our phones, that's it. And courtesy *Por favor*, if you've got a big ass line of homies waiting to use the phone, please, cut it short; let the other homies use the phone too. If both phones are busy, wait. Do not use any of the other phones up in here no matter what. Also, we get the newspaper every morning, the *LA Times* and *La Opinion*, only use our copy which will have our name written in pencil in the top right corner of the front page. Got it!? Good. Moving on.

Time schedule: 5:00 AM is rise and shine; by 5:15 is count time, that means your bunk bed better be done, you need to be posted up front, with your Blues on, shoes on and ready to go. When the deputy walks up in here you need to be lined up with the rest of the homies at an arms distance, with your mouth shut and eyes open so when the deputy calls your name you better have your booking number memorized and speak that shit loud and clear. You fuck up in count time and make the homies look bad and late for chow time and we're going to throw a baby shower for your ass; and if you ain't familiar with a baby shower, boy, keep it that way, trust me on that, homies. Chowtime is at 1, same shit, be dressed and on time, your bunk done. The only time your bunk ain't done is when you're lying in it. Questions? No? Good.

Commissary: we get the order forms Wednesday morning and turn them in in the afternoon; You receive your orders by Friday after chow time. Keep your store safe and don't take anybody else's shit. Any legal paperwork that you may have up in here keep it safe, but if I was you I wouldn't have it up in here cause if it falls into the wrong hands that's on you. Me, personally, I gave consent to my attorney to keep all my shit. Oh, before I forget, one very important thing *Vatos*... Please, please! If you're going to rub one out during shower time please get rid of the evidence. Wash it down the drain, throw it in a towel, keep it in your hand, flush it down the toilet, I don't really give a good fuck what you do with it but don't leave that shit on the walls or on the floor for someone to slip on and shit; another great reason why you must keep your shower shoes on at all times.

Also, if you got kids and they got a birthday coming up and you want to send them a birthday card come talk to me. I got cards for girls and boys; I got all the new shit too: Adventure Time, I got phenius and ferb, some Batman, Spiderman, I got Tinker Bell, all that shit. Also, I got some for moms or for your old lady; I could write their names really nice on it, if you got a picture I can draw a portrait of them too. Also, if you smoke I can get you a square and a match to go with it; 2 soups apiece. If you need anything stronger than tobacco talk to the homie wicked from Pacoima right here. Any questions!? Yes, back there, what up G!? What's your question?

"Yeah, toilet paper homes, where do we get the toilet paper from?"

Good question, if you need TP, toothpaste, shower shoes, extra towels, or you need any personals, come see me at my bunk, I got the TP and all that shit. Did everyone get a fish kit? Make sure you got everything you need in there, sometimes these motherfuckers forget to put a toothbrush or shampoo in there. But if you're missing anything or you need some more soap come see me. And another thing, if you got issues with anybody up in here do not put hands on anyone up in here without checking with me first. Don't take it upon yourselves to move on anybody up in here without clearance; we ain't in the street where you can just act on free will and do your own thing; you're in my house and in my house nobody touches shit without checking with me first. Whatever issues you have in the street, don't worry, they'll be waiting for you when you get out, but as long as you're in my house, all that street bullshit is irrelevant. If you got a *vato* up in here from a barrio you don't get along with or you spot a vato who smoked your homeboy maybe or stabbed your cousin or cheated on your sister or raped your moms and made your pops watch, I don't give a fuck, leave that shit in the street. This is my house and in my house everyone is family, and family got to follow the family rules; I'm the head of household up in this bitch and you will respect my house or suffer the repercussions. Are we clear?... I said, are we clear!? Good. Good. Class dismissed.

...

So. I guess failure is the best teacher. And Uncle Lefty was always good at explaining things. I'm sure whatever Uncle Lefty is up to nowadays he's doing it right.

As I think back and recall these stories, I come to realize that all those characters are reflections of myself.

All of these characters, in some form or another, have been deemed as society's scum. The gang members, the career criminals, convicts, juvenile delinquents, drug addicts, and drug dealers, blue collar workers, low-income residents, the homeless . . . the villains.

I'm wondering, has my whole life been like this? Have I just been treated with suspicion because of how I look or how I speak? I'm thinking of friends I knew with so much potential, yet they never made it out alive. What is wrong with us? Who made us this way? Did we do this to ourselves like they say we did? Or was there some ominous force already at work here? Was our failure preordained? Or did we create this toilsome scenario for ourselves and unknowingly premeditated and eventually manifested our doom?

These villains are not so villainous. Can a villain write a villanelle that can touch your soul? Can a bad guy tell a story that can make you feel his pain or relate to his struggle? If not, then perhaps you are the villain.

By now, most of the people I grew up with are dead or in prison. The few lucky ones that survived are either doing really well or barely living. I am the last of an endangered species.

The last of a dying genre. And for the record, whether someone is known as a villain or hero depends on who is the one telling the story. There are no "heroes" nor "villains," only biased or unbiased storytellers. But we all possess the ability to be heroic in our darkest times or be wicked when they least expect us to. We can all be villainous and heroic, the question is, which one am I? Which one are you?

A Villain's Farewell

This one goes out to my hero
whose ego never had a problem with zero.
The one who's always stood his ground
whether in the mainstream or the underground.
What would you rather be injected with,
pretty poisons or hideous truths?
True villains are out there injecting venom into your dolls.
They have injections falling from the skies and onto their top hats,
they hide their face, they have no face
yet they sit at the front of the table
with their puppets in hand
and their drugs ready to inject.
All hail the hero who refused to be a puppet
even though being a puppet was the coolest shit to be.
Tonight we lay to rest a true friend,
a true villain, this is a villain's farewell.
Tonight, a hero has been born from within us.
One of our own has come back to claim us.
Let us toast to the man who has never been toasted for
who has never been acknowledged
for none other than his mistakes and errors
but never have we looked up and said
brother what can we do for you.
Now we shall redeem ourselves
now that we are empowered ourselves.
Now we shall look out for our brother
who once looked out for us.

Now it is time to unite
now it is time to fight
now it is time to demonstrate our love
and our allegiance and to keep our promise.
For he has given himself to us
and now, we will return the honor.
Cheers to our hero, the Villain.

ACKNOWLEDGMENTS

I would like to thank my friends, family, and supporters who helped make this book possible. To my CLI family, Riot of Roses Publishing House, World Stage Press, Sims Library of Poetry, Anansi Writers Workshop, and to every poet, artist, student, and worker who I had the pleasure of meeting along this journey. To every open mic out there, too many to name. To every author whose book I helped release. To all my homegirls and homeboys who helped me through the pandemic. To my children, you are my strength, my love, my everything.

ABOUT THE AUTHOR

Carlos Ornelas is a Mexican American Poet and Artist from Lynwood in Los Angeles County, California. He is a father and a lover of art. His first book, *Ketchup: Sopa de Gato*, was released in 2013 and has been in Los Angeles classrooms through the Living Writer's Series and is associated with the development of the Community Literature Initiative (CLI) program. Ornelas has been active in the Los Angeles poetry scene for over 20 years and is an active supporter of poetry, music, and art.

Gmail: mr.carlosornelas@gmail.com
Instagram: @carlosornelaspoetry

RIOT OF ROSES
PUBLISHING HOUSE

SEJATNGA
UNCEDED TONGVA TERRITORY
SOUTH WHITTIER, CALIFORNIA

ABOUT THE PUBLISHER

Riot of Roses Publishing House was founded in 2021 specifically to amplify the stories of historically silenced voices.

Xicana owned. Mujerista focused. For the people.

We publish books that heal and liberate.

Read our rebellion.

Web: riotofrosespublishinghouse.com
Instagram: @riotofrosespublishing

9 781961 717114